# baby knits

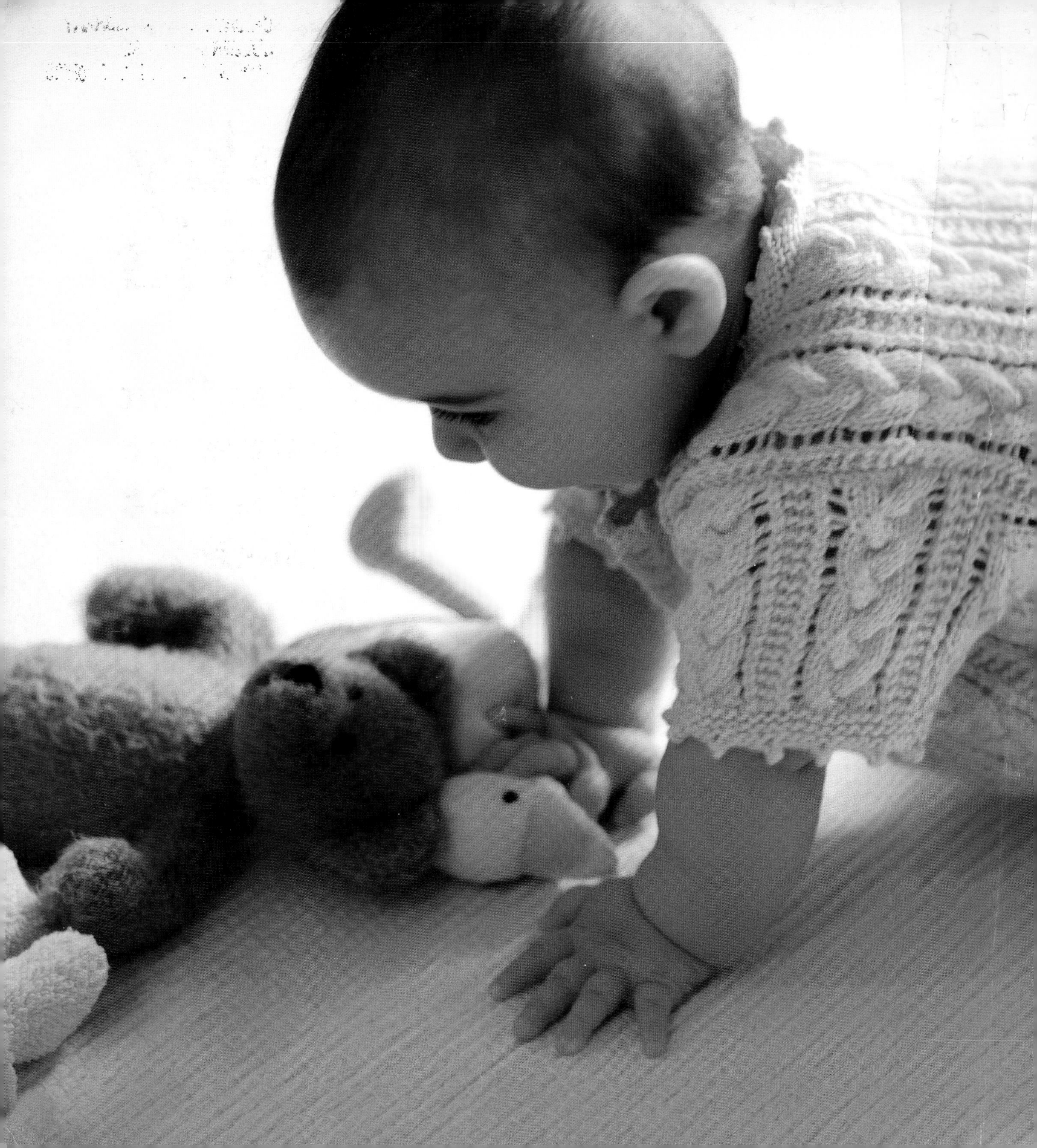

# baby knits

## 20 handknit designs for babies 0-24 months

## Lois Daykin

### PHOTOGRAPHS BY JOHN HESELTINE

St. Martin's Griffin
New York

**BABY KNITS**

www.stmartins.com

*Project editor* Susan Berry
*US editor* Sally Harding
*Designer* Anne Wilson
*Stylist* Susan Berry
*Patterns writing & checking* Sue Whiting,
Tricia McKenzie

Library of Congress Cataloging-in-Publication Data
Available Upon Request

ISBN-10: 0-312-36882-8
ISBN-13: 978-0-312-36882-1

Created by Berry & Co. (Publishing Ltd.) for Rowan Yarns
First U.S. Edition: August 2007

10 9 8 7 6 5 4 3 2 1

Reproduced and printed in Singapore.

# contents

# introduction

• • • • • • • • • •

Everyone wants to knit something for a new baby. It is just about the nicest gift you can give to a much-loved friend or relative to mark such a special occasion, so I have included not only designs you can knit but also ideas for wrapping and presenting your knitted gifts, too.

Rowan has some wonderful new soft and luxurious yarns that are ideal for the delicate skin of a little baby and are easy to wash. They will almost certainly entice you into picking up your needles.

I have chosen a sugar-almond color palette for this book, because it suits the style of the designs and is also very pretty. Some of the designs are for newborns—such as the little bootees, teddy suit, and rompers and hat—while the cardigans and sweaters have been designed with toddlers in mind.

You will find items for boys and girls on the following pages, with traditional color choices, but obviously you can choose unisex colorways, if you prefer. There are a mixture of both garments and accessories, along with some great ideas for the nursery, too. I particularly enjoyed creating the nursery wall hanging and the patchwork-style cushion and blanket.

Many of the projects are simple enough for an inexperienced knitter, while a few will provide more expert ones with a challenge.

# textured jacket

• • • • • • • • • •

Knitted in Rowan *Handknit Cotton*, this little button-up jacket, with its ribbed collar and pockets, is worked in a very simple stitch repeat of narrow panels that create an interesting textured effect. It has been designed to make an outfit for young babies when worn with the stockinette stitch trousers on page 17 and the little pixie hat with tassels on page 20, but it comes in five sizes so that older children can wear it, too. For a more girly look, knit it in lavender or rose.

The jacket is cropped fairly short, but if you want a longer version, simply add a few rows to the pattern after inserting the pocket linings and before you reach the armholes on the back and the fronts.

## To fit age, approximately

| 3–6 | 6–9 | 9–12 | 12–18 | 18–24 | months |
|---|---|---|---|---|---|
| **Finished measurements** | | | | | |
| **AROUND CHEST** | | | | | |
| 20½ | 22 | 23½ | 25½ | 27½ | in |
| 52 | 56 | 60 | 65 | 70 | cm |
| **LENGTH FROM SHOULDER** | | | | | |
| 9½ | 10¼ | 11 | 12½ | 14¼ | in |
| 24 | 26 | 28 | 32 | 36 | cm |
| **SLEEVE SEAM** | | | | | |
| 5 | 6 | 6¾ | 7¾ | 8¾ | in |
| 13 | 15 | 17 | 20 | 22 | cm |

## Yarns

6 (6: 7: 8: 9) x 50g/1¾oz balls of Rowan *Handknit Cotton* in Ice Water 239

## Needles

Pair of size 3 (3.25mm) knitting needles
Pair of size 6 (4mm) knitting needles

## Extras

4 buttons

## Gauge

20 sts and 28 rows to 4in/10cm measured over st st using size 6 (4mm) needles *or size to obtain correct gauge.*

## Abbreviations

See page 117.

## Back

Using size 3 (3.25mm) needles, cast on 55 (59: 63: 67: 71) sts.
**Rib row 1 (RS)** P1, *K1, P1, rep from * to end.
**Rib row 2** K1, *P1, K1, rep from * to end.

These 2 rows form rib.
Work in rib for 4 (4: 4: 6: 6) rows more, ending with RS facing for next row.
Change to size 6 (4mm) needles.
Now work in patt as foll:
**Row 1 (RS)** [P1, K1] 3 (4: 0: 1: 2) times, *P3, [K1, P1] 3 times, K1, rep from * to last 9 (11: 3: 5: 7) sts, P3, [K1, P1] 3 (4: 0: 1: 2) times.
**Row 2** P0 (0: 0: 2: 1), K0 (1: 3: 3: 1), P1 (2: 2: 2: 2), *K1, P1, K1, P2, K3, P2, rep from * to last 4 (6: 8: 10: 7) sts, K1, P1, K1, P1 (2: 2: 2: 2), K0 (1: 3: 3: 1), P0 (0: 0: 2: 1).
These 2 rows form patt.
Work even in patt until Back measures 5½ (6: 6¼: 7½: 8¾)in/14 (15: 16: 19: 22)cm, ending with RS facing for next row.

### SHAPE ARMHOLES

Keeping patt correct, bind off 2 (2: 3: 3: 4) sts at beg of next 2 rows. 51 (55: 57: 61: 63) sts.
Dec 1 st at each end of next row and foll 1 (2: 2: 3: 3) alt rows. 47 (49: 51: 53: 55) sts.
Work even until armhole measures 4 (4¼: 4¾: 5: 5½)in/10 (11: 12: 13: 14)cm, ending with RS facing for next row.

### SHAPE SHOULDERS

Bind off 12 (13: 13: 14: 14) sts at beg of next 2 rows.
Break off yarn and leave rem 23 (23: 25: 25: 27) sts on a holder.

## Pocket linings (make 2)

Using size 6 (4mm) needles, cast on 13 sts.
**Row 1 (RS)** P3, K1, [P1, K1] 3 times, P3.
**Row 2** K3, P2, K1, P1, K1, P2, K3.
These 2 rows form patt.
Work in patt for 13 (13: 15: 15: 17) rows more, ending with WS facing for next row.
Break off yarn and leave sts on a holder.

## Left front

Using size 3 (3.25mm) needles, cast on 33 (35: 37: 39: 41) sts.

**Rib row 1 (RS)** P1, *K1, P1, rep from * to last 2 sts, K2.

**Rib row 2** K1, *P1, K1, rep from * to end.

These 2 rows form rib.

Work in rib for 3 (3: 3: 5: 5) rows more, ending with WS facing for next row.

**Next row (WS)** Rib 7 and slip these 7 sts onto a holder, inc in next st, rib to end. 27 (29: 31: 33: 35) sts.

Change to size 6 (4mm) needles.

Now work in patt as foll:

**Row 1 (RS)** [P1, K1] 0 (0: 0: 1: 2) times, P0 (0: 3: 3: 3), K0 (0: 1: 1: 1), [P1, K1] 12 (13: 12: 12: 12) times, P1, K2.

**Row 2** [P1, K1] 3 times, P2, [K1, P1] 6 times, K1, P2, K1, P1, K1, P1 (2: 2: 2: 2), K0 (1: 3: 3: 3), P0 (0: 0: 2: 2), K0 (0: 0: 0: 1), P0 (0: 0: 0: 1).

These 2 rows form patt.

Work in patt for 12 (12: 14: 14: 16) rows more, ending with RS facing for next row.

### PLACE POCKET

**Next row (RS)** Patt 6 (8: 10: 12: 14) sts, bind off next 13 sts in patt, patt to end.

**Next row** Patt 8 sts, with WS facing patt across 13 sts of first Pocket Lining, patt to end.

Keeping patt correct as now set by Pocket Lining sts, work even in patt until Left Front matches Back to start of armhole shaping, ending with RS facing for next row.

### SHAPE ARMHOLE

Keeping patt correct, bind off 2 (2: 3: 3: 4) sts at beg of next row. 25 (27: 28: 30: 31) sts.

Work 1 row.

Dec 1 st at armhole edge of next row and foll
1 (2: 2: 3: 3) alt rows. 23 (24: 25: 26: 27) sts.
Work even until armhole measures 2 (2¼: 2¼:
2¾: 2¾)in/5 (6: 6: 7: 7)cm, ending with WS
facing for next row.

**SHAPE NECK**

**Next row (WS)** Patt 3 (3: 4: 4: 5) sts and slip
these sts onto a holder, patt to end. 20 (21: 21:
22: 22) sts.

Dec 1 st at neck edge of next 8 rows. 12 (13: 13:
14: 14) sts.

Work even until Left Front matches Back to
shoulder, ending with RS facing for next row.

**SHAPE SHOULDER**

Bind off rem 12 (13: 13: 14: 14) sts.

## Right front

Using size 3 (3.25mm) needles, cast on 33 (35:
37: 39: 41) sts.

**Rib row 1 (RS)** K2, P1, *K1, P1, rep from * to end.

**Rib row 2** K1, *P1, K1, rep from * to end.

These 2 rows form rib.

Work in rib for 3 (3: 3: 5: 5) rows more, ending
with WS facing for next row.

**Next row (WS)** Rib to last 8 sts, inc in next st and
turn, leaving rem 7 sts on a holder. 27 (29: 31:
33: 35) sts.

Change to size 6 (4mm) needles.

Now work in patt as foll:

**Row 1 (RS)** K2, P1, [K1, P1] 12 (13: 12: 12: 12)
times, K0 (0: 1: 1: 1), P0 (0: 3: 3: 3), [K1, P1] 0
(0: 0: 1: 2) times.

**Row 2** P0 (0: 0: 0: 1), K0 (0: 0: 0: 1), P0 (0: 0: 2:
2), K0 (1: 3: 3: 3), P1 (2: 2: 2: 2), K1, P1, K1, P2,
K1, [P1, K1] 6 times, P2, [K1, P1] 3 times.

These 2 rows form patt.

Work in patt for 12 (12: 14: 14: 16) rows more, ending with RS facing for next row.

**PLACE POCKET**

**Next row (RS)** Patt 8 sts, bind off next 13 sts in patt, patt to end.

**Next row** Patt 6 (8: 10: 12: 14) sts, with WS facing patt across 13 sts of second Pocket Lining, patt to end.

Keeping patt correct as now set by Pocket Lining sts, complete to match Left Front, reversing shapings.

## Sleeves

Using size 3 (3.25mm) needles, cast on 35 (35: 39: 39: 43) sts.

Starting with rib row 2, work in rib as given for Back for 6 (6: 6: 8: 8) rows, ending with RS facing for next row.

Change to size 6 (4mm) needles.

Now work in patt as foll:

**Row 1 (RS)** [K1, P1] 0 (0: 1: 1: 2) times, *K1, P3, [K1, P1] 3 times, rep from * to last 5 (5: 7: 7: 9) sts, K1, P3, K1, [P1, K1] 0 (0: 1: 1: 2) times.

**Row 2** [K1, P1] 0 (0: 0: 0: 1) times, K0 (0: 1: 1: 1), P1 (1: 2: 2: 2), *K3, P2, K1, P1, K1, P2, rep from * to last 4 (4: 6: 6: 8) sts, K3, P1 (1: 2: 2: 2), K0 (0: 1: 1: 1), [P1, K1] 0 (0: 0: 0: 1) times.

These 2 rows form patt.

Work in patt, shaping sides by inc 1 st at each end of next row and every foll 4th row until there are 47 (49: 55: 57: 61) sts, taking inc sts into seed st.

Work even until Sleeve measures 5 (6: 6¾: 7¾: 8¾)in/ 13 (15: 17: 20: 22)cm, ending with RS facing for next row.

**SHAPE TOP**

Keeping patt correct, bind off 2 (2: 3: 3: 4) sts at beg of next 2 rows. 43 (45: 49: 51: 53) sts.

Dec 1 st at each end of next row and foll 1 (2: 2: 3: 3) alt rows.

Work 1 row, ending with RS facing for next row.

Bind off rem 39 (39: 43: 43: 45) sts.

## Finishing

Press lightly on WS following instructions on yarn label.
Sew both shoulder seams.

**BUTTON BAND**

**GIRL'S VERSION ONLY**

Slip 7 sts from left front holder onto size 3 (3.25mm) needles and rejoin yarn with RS facing, inc in first st, rib to end. 8 sts.

**BOY'S VERSION ONLY**

Slip 7 sts from right front holder onto size 3 (3.25mm) needles and rejoin yarn with WS facing, inc in first st, rib to end. 8 sts.

**BOTH VERSIONS**

Work in rib as set until Band, when slightly stretched, fits up front opening edge to neck shaping, ending with RS facing for next row.

Break off yarn and leave sts on a holder.

Slip stitch Band in place.

Mark positions for 4 buttons on this band—first to come 2¼in/ 6cm up from cast-on edge, last to come 1in/2.5cm below neck shaping and rem 2 buttons evenly spaced between.

**BUTTONHOLE BAND**

**GIRL'S VERSION ONLY**

Slip 7 sts from right front holder onto size 3 (3.25mm) needles and rejoin yarn with WS facing, inc in first st, rib to end. 8 sts.

**BOY'S VERSION ONLY**

Slip 7 sts from left front holder onto size 3 (3.25mm) needles and rejoin yarn with RS facing, inc in first st, rib to end. 8 sts.

**BOTH VERSIONS**

Work in rib as set until Band, when slightly stretched, fits up front opening edge to neck shaping, ending with RS facing for next row **and at the same time** work 4 buttonholes to correspond with positions marked for buttons as foll:

**Buttonhole row (RS)** Rib 3, work 2 tog, yo (to make a

buttonhole), rib 3.

When Band is complete, break off yarn and leave sts on a holder.

Slip stitch Band in place.

**Collar**

With RS facing and using size 3 (3.25mm) needles, rib first 7 sts of right front Band, work tog last st of Band with first st on right front holder, K rem 2 (2: 3: 3: 4) sts on right front holder, pick up and knit 17 (17: 19: 19: 21) sts up right side of neck, K across 23 (23: 25: 25: 27) sts on back holder, pick up and knit 17 (17: 19: 19: 21) sts down left side of neck, then K first 2 (2: 3: 3: 4) sts on left front holder, work tog last st on left front holder with first st of left front Band, rib rem 7 sts of left front Band. 77 (77: 85: 85: 93) sts.

Working all sts in rib as set by Bands, work in rib for 1 row, ending with RS of body (WS of Collar) facing for next row.

**Next row** Rib to last 26 (26: 28: 28: 30) sts and turn.

Rep last row once more.

**Next row** Rib to last 21 (21: 22: 22: 23) sts and turn.

Rep last row once more.

**Next row** Rib to last 16 sts and turn.

Rep last row once more.

**Next row** Rib to end.

Work in rib across all sts for 3 rows.

Bind off 5 sts at beg of next 2 rows. 67 (67: 75: 75: 83) sts.

Work in rib for 10 (10: 12: 12: 14) rows more.

Bind off in rib.

Matching shaped edges at underarm and center of sleeve bound-off edge to shoulder seam, sew Sleeves into armholes. Sew side and sleeve seams. Sew Pocket Linings in place on inside. Sew on buttons.

# drawstring trousers

• • • • • • • • •

These simple stockinette stitch trousers, knitted in Rowan *Handknit Cotton*, are roomy enough to slide easily over diapers, and stretchy enough for your baby to feel comfortable no matter how much they crawl around. If you prefer, you can make a knitted cord with a knitting spool for the waistband instead of threading elastic through it as recommended. The little ribbed top pocket at the back of the trousers is optional.

The trousers are intended for young babies (from 3 to 12 months) only. To make a complete outfit, knit them in matching blue yarn and team them with the jacket on page 8.

*gallery of projects*

## To fit age, approximately

| 3–6 | 6–9 | 9–12 | months |
|---|---|---|---|

### Finished measurements

**AROUND HIP**

| 18 | 20 | 22 | in |
|---|---|---|---|
| 46 | 51 | 56 | cm |

**LENGTH FROM WAIST**

| 13 | 15 | 17 | in |
|---|---|---|---|
| 33 | 38 | 43 | cm |

## Yarns

4 (4: 5) x 50g/1¾oz balls of Rowan *Handknit Cotton* in **MC** (Ice Water 239 or Linen 205), and 1 ball in **CC** (Linen 205 or Ice Water 239)

## Needles

Pair of size 3 (3.25mm) knitting needles
Pair of size 6 (4mm) knitting needles

## Extras

Waist length of ¾in/2cm wide elastic

## Gauge

20 sts and 28 rows to 4in/10cm measured over st st using size 6 (4mm) needles *or size to obtain correct gauge.*

## Abbreviations

See page 117.

## Legs (make 2)

Using size 6 (4mm) needles and CC, cast on 54 (60: 66) sts.
Starting with a P row, work in st st for 3 rows, ending with RS facing for next row.
Join in MC.
Using MC, work 1 row.
Using CC, work 3 rows.
Break off CC and cont using MC only.

Work 1 row, ending with WS facing for next row.

**Next row (WS)** Knit (to form fold line).

Starting with a K row, work in st st for 8 rows.

**Next row (RS)** Purl.

Change to size 6 (4mm) needles.

Starting with a P row, work in st st until Leg measures 6¼ (6¾: 7½)in/16 (17: 19)cm from fold line row, ending with RS facing for next row.

**SHAPE FOR CROTCH**

Inc 1 st at each end of next row and foll 2 (2: 3) alt rows. 60 (66: 74) sts.

Work 1 row, ending with RS facing for next row.

Cast on 3 sts at beg of next 2 rows. 66 (72: 80) sts.

**SHAPE FOR LEG**

Dec 1 st at each end of 3rd row and foll 2 (3: 4) alt rows, then on every foll 6th row until 48 (52: 56) sts rem.

Work 3 (5: 7) rows, dec 1 st at end of last row and ending with RS facing for next row. 47 (51: 55) sts.

Change to size 3 (3.25mm) needles and work cuff ribbing as foll:

**Rib row 1 (RS)** K1, *P1, K1, rep from * to end.

**Rib row 2** P1, *K1, P1, rep from * to end.

These 2 rows form rib.

Work in rib for 2 (2: 4) rows more, ending with RS facing for next row.

Bind off in rib.

### Pocket

Using size 3 (3.25mm) needles and MC, cast on 13 (15: 15) sts.

Work 4 (4: 6) rows in rib as for cuff on Legs.

Starting with a K row work 12 (12: 14) rows in st st, ending with RS facing for next row.

**Next row (dec row) (RS)** K1, skp, K to last 3 sts, K2tog, K1. 11 (13: 13) sts.

Purl 1 row.

Rep last 2 rows once more, then first of last 2 rows (the dec row) again.

Bind off rem 7 (9: 9) sts purlwise.

### Finishing

Press lightly on WS following instructions on yarn label.

Sew inside leg seams. Sew Legs together along front and back crotch seam. Fold first 8 rows to inside along fold line row and slip stitch in place to form waistband casing, leaving an opening. Thread elastic through opening, sew together ends and then sew casing opening closed.

# pixie hat

• • • • • • • • •

This little hat has been knitted in Rowan *Handknit Cotton* using blue and beige colorways, like the trousers on page 17 and the jacket on page 8, to complete the matching outfit for babies from 3 to 12 months old. The ribbed band is knitted in the contrasting color and rolls up to form a brim. A tassel at each of the two corners of the hat adds a cute finishing touch.

Because it requires no shaping whatsoever, this is a very easy hat pattern. Even beginner knitters will have no difficulty with this one! It would make an ideal first project to knit and a great gift for a young baby.

**To fit age, approximately**

| 3–6 | 6–9 | 9–12 | months |
|---|---|---|---|

**Finished measurements**

**CIRCUMFERENCE AROUND HEAD**

| 13¼ | 14 | 15¼ | in |
|---|---|---|---|
| 34 | 36 | 39 | cm |

## Yarns

1 x 50g/1¾oz ball of Rowan *Handknit Cotton* in each of
**MC** (Ice Water 239) and **CC** (Linen 205)

## Needles

Pair of size 3 (3.25mm) knitting needles
Pair of size 6 (4mm) knitting needles

## Gauge

20 sts and 28 rows to 4in/10cm measured over st st using
size 6 (4mm) needles *or size to obtain correct gauge.*

## Abbreviations

See page 117.

## Hat

Using size 3 (3.25mm) needles and CC, cast on 68 (72:
78) sts.
**Row 1 (RS)** *K1, P1, rep from * to end.
**Rows 2 to 4** As row 1.
Change to size 6 (4mm) needles.
Starting with a K row, work in st st for 7 rows, ending with
WS facing for next row.
**Row 12 (WS)** Knit (to form fold line).
**Row 13** Knit.
Join in MC.
Starting with a K row (to reverse RS of work), work in striped
st st as foll:
Using MC, work 3 rows.

*gallery of projects*

Using CC, work 1 row.
These 4 rows form striped st st.
Work in striped st st until Hat
measures 5½ (6: 6¼)in/14 (15:
16)cm from fold line row, ending with
RS facing for next row.
Bind off.

## Finishing
Press lightly on WS following
instructions on yarn label.
Sew row-end edges together to form
back seam, reversing seam for first 11
rows for turn-back. Positioning seam
centrally on "tube," sew bound-off
edges together to form top seam.
Using CC, make two 3in/8cm long
tassels and sew one to each top
corner of Hat as in photograph.

# rabbit

• • • • • • • • • •

Everyone enjoys finding a really sweet toy to knit, and this enchanting rabbit, with its long floppy bunny ears and its pretty Fair Isle style dress with a pink ribbon detail, is just the thing. Knitted in Rowan *Cashsoft Baby DK*, the toy feels wonderfully soft to the touch—exactly what any child wants to cuddle.

Both the rabbit and its dress are for intermediate or experienced knitters and are well worth the time and effort, as the toy was a great hit with our young models. Slightly older toddlers will enjoy dressing and undressing the rabbit, too.

## Size
Finished rabbit is approximately 9¾in/25cm tall, excluding ears.

## Yarns
**RABBIT**
2 x 50g/1¾oz balls of Rowan *RYC Cashsoft Baby DK* in Crocus 808
**DRESS**
1 x 50g/1¾oz ball of Rowan *RYC Cashsoft 4 ply* in each of **A** (Mosaic 426), **C** (Ginger 435), and **E** (Spring 428)
1 x 50g/1¾oz ball of Rowan *4 ply Soft* in each of **B** (Victoria 390) and **D** (Folly 391)

## Needles
Pair of size 3 (3.25mm) knitting needles

## Extras
**RABBIT**
Washable toy filling
2 buttons (for eyes)
Scraps of brown and cream yarn (for face)
**DRESS**
1 button
35¼in/90cm of ⅜in/1cm wide ribbon

## Gauge
**RABBIT**
24 sts and 34 rows to 4in/10cm measured over st st using size 3 (3.25mm) needles *or size to obtain correct gauge.*
**DRESS**
28 sts and 36 rows to 4in/10cm measured over st st using size 3 (3.25mm) needles *or size to obtain correct gauge.*

## Abbreviations
See page 117.

# rabbit

## Body
Using size 3 (3.25mm) needles, cast on 15 sts.
Starting with a K row, work in st st as foll:
Knit 1 row.
**Row 2 (WS)** [P1, M1, P6, M1] twice, P1. 19 sts.
**Row 3** K1, M1, K3, [M1, K1, M1, K4] twice, M1, K1, M1, K3, M1, K1. 27 sts.
**Row 4** [P1, M1, P12, M1] twice, P1. 31 sts.
**Row 5** K1, M1, K6, [M1, K1, M1, K7] twice, M1, K1, M1, K6, M1, K1. 39 sts.
Work 1 row.
**Row 7** [K1, M1, K18, M1] twice, K1. 43 sts.
Work 3 rows.
**Row 11** K21, M1, K1, M1, K21. 45 sts.
Work 13 rows.
**Row 25** K20, K2tog, K1, skp, K20. 43 sts.
Work 3 rows.
**Row 29** [K1, skp, K16, K2tog] twice, K1. 39 sts.
Work 3 rows.
**Row 33** [K1, skp, K14, K2tog] twice, K1. 35 sts.
Work 3 rows.
**Row 37** [K1, skp, K12, K2tog] twice, K1. 31 sts.
Work 1 row.
**Row 39** K1, skp, K2, [K2tog, K1, skp, K3] twice, K2tog, K1, skp, K2, K2tog, K1. 23 sts.
Work 1 row.
**Row 41** K1, skp, [K2tog, K1, skp, K1] twice, K2tog, K1, skp, K2tog, K1. 15 sts.
Work 1 row.
**Row 43** [K1, skp, K2, K2tog] twice, K1. 11 sts.
**Row 44** [P1, P2tog, P2tog tbl] twice, P1.
Break off yarn and thread through rem 7 sts. Pull up tight and fasten off securely.
Sew back seam. Insert toy filling so Body is firmly filled. Run

a gathering thread around cast-on edge, pull up tight, and fasten off securely.

## Head

Using size 3 (3.25mm) needles, cast on 30 sts.
Starting with a K row, work in st st as foll:
Work 2 rows.
**Row 3 (RS)** K13, M1, K4, M1, K13. 32 sts.
**Row 4** P1, M1, P11, M1, P8, M1, P11, M1, P1. 36 sts.
**Row 5** K15, M1, K6, M1, K15. 38 sts.
**Row 6** P1, M1, P36, M1, P1. 40 sts.
**Row 7** Cast on 4 sts, K until there are 20 sts on right needle, M1, K8, M1, K to end. 46 sts.
**Row 8** Cast on 4 sts, P to end. 50 sts.
**Row 9** K1, M1, K18, M1, K12, M1, K18, M1, K1. 54 sts.
**Row 10** P1, M1, P52, M1, P1. 56 sts.
**Row 11** K23, M1, K10, M1, K23. 58 sts.
Work 5 rows.
**Row 17** K23, M1, K12, M1, K23. 60 sts.
Work 1 row.
Place a marker at each end of last row.
**Row 19** K1, skp, K54, K2tog, K1. 58 sts.
**Row 20** P1, P2tog, P52, P2tog tbl, P1. 56 sts.
**Row 21** K1, skp, K16, K2tog, K14, skp, K16, K2tog, K1. 52 sts.
**Row 22** P1, P2tog, P14, P2tog tbl, P14, P2tog, P14, P2tog tbl, P1. 48 sts.
**Row 23** K1, skp, K12, K2tog, K14, skp, K12, K2tog, K1. 44 sts.
**Row 24** P1, P2tog, P10, P2tog tbl, P14, P2tog, P10, P2tog tbl, P1. 40 sts.
**Row 25** K1, skp, K8, K2tog, K14, skp, K8, K2tog, K1. 36 sts.
**Row 26** P1, P2tog, P6, P2tog tbl, P14, P2tog, P6, P2tog tbl, P1. 32 sts.
Bind off 8 sts at beg of next 2 rows. 16 sts.
**Row 29** K1, skp, K10, K2tog, K1. 14 sts.

Work 3 rows.
**Row 33** K1, skp, K8, K2tog, K1. 12 sts.
Work 3 rows.
**Row 37** K1, skp, K6, K2tog, K1. 10 sts.
**Row 38** P1, P2tog, P4, P2tog tbl, P1. 8 sts.
Work 6 rows.
**Row 45** K1, skp, K2, K2tog, K1. 6 sts.
Work 3 rows.
**Row 49** K1, skp, K2tog, K1. 4 sts.
**Row 50** P2tog tbl, P2tog.
**Row 51** K2tog and fasten off.
Sew together row-end edges from cast-on edge to markers to form chin seam. Matching fasten-off point to top of chin seam, sew row-end edges of gusset section to shaped row-end and bound-off edges of front of Head. Insert toy filling. Sew Head to top of Body as in photograph, matching back seam of Body to center of cast-on edge of Head and inserting a little more toy filling if required.

## Legs (make 2)

Using size 3 (3.25mm) needles, cast on 39 sts.
Starting with a K row, work in st st as foll:
Work 6 rows.
**Row 7 (RS)** K17, K2tog, K1, skp, K17. 37 sts.
**Row 8** P16, P2tog tbl, P1, P2tog, P16. 35 sts.
**Row 9** K15, K2tog, K1, skp, K15. 33 sts.
**Row 10** P12, bind off next 9 sts, P to end. 24 sts.
**Row 11** K11, K2tog, K11. 23 sts.
**Row 12** P9, P2tog tbl, P1, P2tog, P9. 21 sts.
Work 2 rows.
**Row 15** [K1, M1, K9, M1] twice, K1. 25 sts.
Work 3 rows.
**Row 19** K12, M1, K1, M1, K12. 27 sts.
Work 13 rows.
**Row 33** K11, K2tog, K1, skp, K11. 25 sts.
Work 1 row.

**Row 35** [K1, skp, K7, K2tog] twice, K1.
21 sts.
Work 1 row.
**Row 37** [K1, skp, K5, K2tog] twice, K1.
17 sts.
**Row 38** [P1, P2tog, P3, P2tog tbl]
twice, P1.
Bind off rem 13 sts.
Sew top seam of foot section. Sew
together bound-off and row-end
edges, leaving cast-on edge open.
Insert toy filling.

**Soles** (make 2)
Using size 3 (3.25mm) needles, cast
on 5 sts.
**Row 1 (RS)** [K1, P1] twice, K1.
**Row 2** Inc in first st, P1, K1, P1, inc in
last st. 7 sts.
These 2 rows form seed st and start
shaping.
Keeping seed st correct, inc 1 st at each
end of next row and foll alt row. 11 sts.
Work 11 rows.
Dec 1 st at each end of next row and
foll alt row, then on foll row, ending
with RS facing for next row.
Bind off rem 5 sts.
Sew Sole to cast-on edge of Leg,
inserting a little more toy filling into
Leg if required. Sew bound-off edges
of Legs to base of Body.

**Arms** (make 2)
Using size 3 (3.25mm) needles, cast
on 15 sts.

Starting with a K row, work in st st as foll:

Work 1 row.

**Row 2 (WS)** [P1, M1, P6, M1] twice, P1. 19 sts.

**Row 3** [K1, M1, K8, M1] twice, K1. 23 sts.

**Row 4** [P1, M1, P10, M1] twice, P1. 27 sts.

**Row 5** K1, M1, K25, M1, K1. 29 sts.

Work 1 row.

**Row 7** K1, M1, K27, M1, K1. 31 sts.

Work 1 row.

**Row 9** K1, M1, K12, K2tog, K1, skp, K12, M1, K1. 31 sts.

Work 1 row.

**Row 11** K13, K2tog, K1, skp, K13. 29 sts.

**Row 12** P12, P2tog tbl, P1, P2tog, P12. 27 sts.

**Row 13** K1, M1, K10, K2tog, K1, skp, K10, M1, K1. 27 sts.

**Row 14** P11, P2tog tbl, P1, P2tog, P11. 25 sts.

Work 6 rows.

**Row 21** K12, M1, K1, M1, K12. 27 sts.

Work 11 rows.

**Row 33** K11, K2tog, K1, skp, K11. 25 sts.

Work 3 rows.

**Row 37** [K1, skp, K7, K2tog] twice, K1. 21 sts.

Work 1 row.

**Row 39** [K1, skp, K5, K2tog] twice, K1. 17 sts.

**Row 40** [P1, P2tog, P3, P2tog tbl] twice, P1.

Bind off rem 13 sts.

Sew together cast-on and row-end edges, leaving bound-off edges open. Insert toy filling. Sew bound-off edges of Arms to sides of Body.

**Ears** (make 4 pieces)

Using size 3 (3.25mm) needles, cast on 5 sts.

**Row 1 (RS)** [K1, P1] twice, K1.

**Row 2** As row 1.

These 2 rows form seed st.

Keeping seed st correct, inc 1 st at each end of 3rd row and every foll 6th row until there are 13 sts.

Work 11 rows.

Dec 1 st at each end of next row and foll alt row, then on foll 3 rows, ending with RS facing for next row.

Bind off rem 3 sts.

Join pairs of Ear pieces, leaving cast-on edge open. Make a small pleat in cast-on edge, then sew Ears to Head as in photograph.

**Finishing**

Using photograph as a guide, sew on buttons for eyes. Using scrap of cream yarn, work stem stitch lines above buttons as in photograph. Using scrap of brown yarn, embroider satin stitch nose, then embroider backstitch mouth below nose.

## dress

**Main section**

Using size 3 (3.25mm) needles and A, cast on 109 sts.

Work in garter st (K every row) for 5 rows, ending with WS facing for next row.

**Row 6 (WS)** *P2tog, yo, rep from * to last st, P1.

**Rows 7 and 8** Knit.

Starting and ending rows as indicated, joining in and breaking off colors as required, and repeating the 4-st patt rep 27 times across rows, work 4 rows following chart A (see page 30), ending with RS facing for next row.

**Row 13 (RS)** Knit.

**Rows 14 to 16** Purl.

**Row 17** K1, *yo, K2tog, rep from * to end.

**Rows 18 to 20** Purl.

Starting and ending rows as indicated, joining in and breaking off colors as required, and repeating the 12-st patt rep 9 times across rows, work 14 rows following chart B (see page 30), ending with RS facing for next row.

**Rows 35 to 37** Knit.

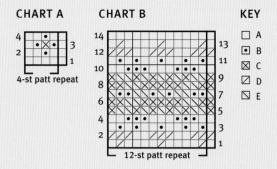

**CHART A**

4-st patt repeat

**CHART B**

12-st patt repeat

**KEY**

☐ A
⊡ B
⊠ C
☑ D
◹ E

**Rows 38 to 40** As rows 6 to 8.

Starting and ending rows as indicated, joining in and breaking off colors as required, and repeating the 4-st patt rep 27 times across rows, work 4 rows following chart A, ending with RS facing for next row.

**Row 45** Knit.

**Row 46** [P2tog] 22 times, [P3tog] 7 times, [P2tog] 22 times. 51 sts.

**Rows 47 and 48** Purl.

**Rows 49 to 52** As rows 17 to 20.

Break off contrasting colors and cont using A only.

Place a marker at each end of last row.

Starting with a K row, work in st st as foll:

**SHAPE LEFT BACK**

**Next row (RS)** K11 and turn, leaving rem sts on a holder.

Work on these 11 sts only for left back.

**Next row (WS)** P1, P2tog, P7, K1. 10 sts.

**Next row** K7, K2tog, K1. 9 sts.

**Next row** P8, K1.

**Next row** Knit.

Rep last 2 rows 3 times more, then first of these rows again.

**SHAPE BACK NECK**

**Next row** K5 and slip these sts onto another holder, K to end. 4 sts.

Dec 1 st at neck edge of next row.

Bind off rem 3 sts.

**SHAPE FRONT**

Rejoin yarn to sts left on first holder, bind off 4 sts, K until there are 21 sts on right needle and turn, leaving rem sts on holder.

Work on these 21 sts only for front.

**Next row (WS)** P1, P2tog, P15, P2tog tbl, P1. 19 sts.

**Next row** K1, skp, K13, K2tog, K1. 17 sts.

**Next row** Purl.

**Next row** Knit.

Rep last 2 rows twice more, then first of these rows again.

**SHAPE FRONT NECK**

**Next row** K5 and turn.

Work on these 5 sts only for first side of neck.

Dec 1 st at neck edge of next 2 rows. 3 sts.

Work 1 row, ending with RS facing for next row.

Bind off rem 3 sts.

Return to sts left before shaping neck, slip center 7 sts onto another holder, K to end. 5 sts.

Dec 1 st at neck edge of next 2 rows. 3 sts.

Work 1 row, ending with RS facing for next row.

Bind off rem 3 sts.

**SHAPE RIGHT BACK**

Rejoin yarn to sts left on first holder, bind off 4 sts, K to end. 11 sts.

Work on these 11 sts for right back.

**Next row (WS)** K1, P7, P2tog tbl, P1. 10 sts.

**Next row** K1, skp, K7. 9 sts.

**Next row** K1, P8.

**Next row** Knit.

Rep last 2 rows 3 times more, then first of these rows again.

**SHAPE BACK NECK**

**Next row** K4 and turn, leaving rem 5 sts on another holder. 4 sts.

Dec 1 st at neck edge of next row.

Bind off rem 3 sts.

## Finishing

Sew back seam below markers.

**ARMHOLE BORDERS** (both alike)

With RS facing, using size 3 (3.25mm) needles and A, pick up and knit 26 sts evenly around entire armhole edge. Work in garter st for 2 rows. Bind off knitwise (on WS). Join shoulder seams.

**NECKBAND**

With RS facing, using size 3 (3.25mm) needles and A, slip 5 sts from left back neck holder onto right needle, pick up and knit 2 sts up left side of back neck, and 4 sts down left side of front neck, K7 sts from front neck holder, pick up and knit 4 sts up right side of front neck, and 2 sts down right side of back neck, then K5 sts from left back neck holder. 29 sts.

**Row 1 (WS)** Knit.

**Row 2** K2tog, yo (to make a buttonhole), K to end.

Bind off knitwise (on WS).

Sew on button to correspond with buttonhole in row 2 of Neckband. Thread ribbon through eyelet holes near armhole edges and tie in a bow at center front.

# cable and lace
# all-in-one

• • • • • • • • • •

Knit this delightful cable and lace pattern to show off your knitting skills. It is worked here in a pretty, soft yellow—suitably unisex if the future baby's sex is not yet known.

Beautifully soft to the touch in Rowan's machine-washable *Cashcotton*, the lacy panels and short sleeves and legs ensure that baby will stay comfortably cool in this very practical all-in-one suit. The cable and lace stitch combination is very stretchy, making it an easy fit. A pretty picot edge circles the neck, sleeves, and legs.

A button opening at the crotch makes for speedy diaper changes with minimum fuss.

## To fit age, approximately

| 3 | 6 | 9 | months |
|---|---|---|---|

## Finished measurements

### AROUND CHEST

| 23½ | 25½ | 27½ | in |
|---|---|---|---|
| 60 | 65 | 70 | cm |

### LENGTH FROM SHOULDER

| 15½ | 18 | 20½ | in |
|---|---|---|---|
| 40 | 46 | 52 | cm |

### SLEEVE SEAM

| 2¼ | 2¼ | 2¼ | in |
|---|---|---|---|
| 6 | 6 | 6 | cm |

## Yarns

3 (4: 5) x 50g/1¾oz balls of Rowan *RYC Cashcotton 4 ply* in Limone 907

## Needles

Pair of size 2 (3mm) knitting needles
Pair of size 3 (3.25mm) knitting needles
Cable needle

## Extras

7 small buttons

## Gauge

28 sts and 36 rows to 4in/10cm measured over st st using size 3 (3.25mm) needles *or size to obtain correct gauge.*

## Abbreviations

**C6B** = slip next 3 sts onto cable needle and leave at back of work, K3, then K3 from cable needle; **C6F** = slip next 3 sts onto cable needle and leave at front of work, K3, then K3 from cable needle.
See also page 117.

## Back

### FIRST LEG

Using size 3 (3.25mm) needles, cast on 43 (47: 51) sts.
Work in patt as foll:
**Row 1 and every foll alt row (WS)** K1 (2: 3), *P2tog, yo, P11, K1 (2: 3), rep from * to end.
**Row 2** K1 (2: 3), *skp, yo, C6B, K6 (7: 8), rep from * to end.
**Row 4** K1 (2: 3), *skp, yo, K12 (13: 14), rep from * to end.
**Row 6** K1 (2: 3), *skp, yo, K3, C6F, K3 (4: 5), rep from * to end.
**Row 8** As row 4.
These 8 rows form patt.
Work in patt for 8 rows more, ending with WS facing for next row.**
Break off yarn and leave sts on a holder.

### SECOND LEG

Work as given for First Leg to **.

### JOIN LEGS

**Next row (WS)** Patt 43 (47: 51) sts of Second Leg, cast on 13 sts onto right needle, then with WS still facing, patt 43 (47: 51) sts of First Leg. 99 (107: 115) sts.
Work in patt until Back measures 8¾ (10¼: 11¾)in/ 22 (26: 30)cm from joining row, ending with RS facing for next row.

### SHAPE ARMHOLES

Keeping patt correct, bind off 8 (9: 10) sts at beg of next 2 rows. 83 (89: 95) sts.
Dec 1 st at each end of next row and foll 5 alt rows. 71 (77: 83) sts.
Work even until armhole measures 3½ (4¼: 5)in/9 (11: 13)cm, ending with RS facing for next row.

### SHAPE BACK NECK

**Next row (RS)** Patt 20 (22: 24) sts and turn, leaving rem sts on a holder.
Work each side of neck separately.
Keeping patt correct, dec 1 st at neck edge of next 4 rows.

16 (18: 20) sts.

Work 3 rows, ending with RS facing for next row.

**SHAPE SHOULDER**

Bind off.

With RS facing, slip center 31 (33: 35) sts onto a holder, rejoin yarn to rem sts, patt to end.

Keeping patt correct, dec 1 st at neck edge of next 4 rows. 16 (18: 20) sts.

Work 2 rows, ending with WS facing for next row.

**SHAPE SHOULDER BUTTON BORDER**

Work in garter st (K every row) for 5 rows, ending with RS facing for next row.

Bind off.

### Front

Work as given for Back until 8 rows less have been worked than on Back to start of back neck shaping, ending with RS facing for next row.

**SHAPE FRONT NECK**

**Next row (RS)** Patt 25 (27: 29) sts and turn, leaving rem sts on a holder.

Work each side of neck separately.

Continuing to work in patt, dec 1 st at neck edge of next 9 rows. 16 (18: 20) sts.

Work 5 rows, ending with WS facing for next row.

**SHAPE SHOULDER BUTTONHOLE BORDER**

**Next row (WS)** Knit.

**Next row** K2, *yo, K2tog, K5 (6: 7), rep from * once more.

Work in garter st for 3 rows more, ending with RS facing for next row.

Bind off.

With RS facing, slip center 21 (23: 25) sts onto a holder, rejoin yarn to rem sts, patt to end.

Keeping patt correct, dec 1 st at neck edge of next 9 rows. 16 (18: 20) sts.

Work 6 rows, ending with RS facing for next row.

**SHAPE SHOULDER**
Bind off.

## Sleeves
Using size 3 (3.25mm) needles, cast on 71 (77: 83) sts.
Work in patt as given for First Leg of Back for 17 rows, ending with RS facing for next row.

**SHAPE TOP OF SLEEVE**
Keeping patt correct, bind off 8 (9: 10) sts at beg of next 2 rows. 55 (59: 63) sts.
Dec 1 st at each end of next row and foll 5 alt rows.
Work 1 row, ending with RS facing for next row.
Bind off rem 43 (47: 51) sts.

## Finishing
Press lightly on WS following instructions on yarn label.
Sew right shoulder seam.

**NECKBAND**
With RS facing and using size 2 (3mm) needles, starting and ending at bound-off edges of shoulder borders, pick up and knit 16 sts down left side of front neck, work across 21 (23: 25) sts on front holder as foll: K7 (8: 9), [K2tog, K1] twice, K2tog, K6 (7: 8), pick up and knit 14 sts up right side of front neck, and 7 sts down right side of back neck, then work across 31 (33: 35) sts on back holder as foll: [K1, K2tog] twice, K6 (7: 8), [K2tog, K1] twice, K2tog, K6 (7: 8), K2tog, K1, K2tog, then pick up and knit 9 sts up left side of back neck. 88 (92: 96) sts.
**Row 1 (WS)** Knit.
**Row 2** K1, K2tog, yo, K to end.
Work in garter st for 3 rows more, ending with RS facing for next row.
Work picot bind-off as foll: bind off 3 sts (one st on right needle), *slip st on right needle back onto left needle, cast on 2 sts onto left needle, bind off 6 sts (one st on right needle), rep from * to end, ending last rep by binding off 7 sts.

### CUFF EDGINGS (both alike)

With RS facing and using size 2 (3mm) needles, pick up and knit 59 (67: 75) sts along cast-on edge of Sleeve.

Work in garter st for 5 rows, ending with RS facing for next row.

Work picot bind-off as foll: bind off 3 sts (one st on right needle), *slip st on right needle back onto left needle, cast on 2 sts onto left needle, bind off 6 sts (one st on right needle), rep from * to end.

Lay front shoulder buttonhole border over back shoulder button border and sew together at armhole edge. Matching shaped edges at underarm and center of sleeve bound-off edge to shoulder seam, sew Sleeves to Back and Front. Sew side and sleeve seams.

### HEM EDGINGS (both alike)

With RS facing and using size 2 (3mm) needles, pick up and knit 59 (67: 75) sts along entire cast-on edge of one leg section.

Work in garter st for 5 rows, ending with RS facing for next row.

Work picot bind-off as given for Cuff Edgings.

### BACK INSIDE LEG BUTTON BORDER

With RS facing and using size 2 (3mm) needles, starting and ending at bound-off edges of Hem Edgings, pick up and knit 12 sts up first row-end edge, 10 sts from cast-on edge between legs, the 12 sts down other row-end edge. 34 sts.

Work in garter st for 5 rows, ending with RS facing for next row.

Bind off.

### FRONT INSIDE LEG BUTTONHOLE BORDER

Work as given for Back Inside Leg Button Border, making buttonholes in row 3 as foll:

**Row 3 (WS)** K3, [yo, K2tog, K7] 3 times, yo, K2tog, K2.

Sew on buttons to correspond with buttonholes.

*cable and lace all-in-one*

# bootees

• • • • • • • • •

These bootees are knitted in Rowan *Calmer*, a soft wool/cotton mix yarn ideal for a little baby's sensitive feet. The colorways match those of the jacket, trousers, and hat combination shown on pages 8, 17, and 20, so you can make them to go with the outfit. The ribbed cuff in the contrasting color splits at the ankle to ensure a comfy fit for even the plumpest little legs. A fine stripe adds a stylish detail to the toe of the bootee.

Baby bootees take no time at all to knit, and are a great gift for a new baby. Because they take very little yarn, you can make them from leftover yarn if you wish, but be sure to test the gauge first.

## To fit age, approximately

| 0–3 | 3–6 | 6–9 | months |
|-----|-----|-----|--------|

### Finished measurements

**LENGTH OF FOOT**

| 2¾ | 3¼ | 3¾ | in |
|----|----|----|----|
| 7 | 8.5 | 9.5 | cm |

## Yarns

1 x 50g/1¾oz ball of Rowan *Calmer* in each of **MC** (Calmer 463) and **CC** (Calm 461)

## Needles

Pair of size 7 (4.5mm) knitting needles

## Gauge

22 sts and 32 rows to 4in/10cm measured over st st using size 7 (4.5mm) needles *or size to obtain correct gauge.*

## Abbreviations

See page 117.

## Soles (make 2)

Using size 7 (4.5mm) needles and MC, cast on 3 (5: 7) sts. (This edge forms back edge of heel.)

**Row 1 (WS)** Purl.

**Row 2** K1, M1, K1 (3: 5), M1, K1. 5 (7: 9) sts.

**Row 3** P1, M1P, P to last st, M1P, P1. 7 (9: 11) sts.

**Row 4** Knit.

**Row 5** As row 3. 9 (11: 13) sts.

Starting with a K row, work in st st for 4 (6: 8) rows, ending with RS facing for next row.

Place a marker at each end of last row.

Work 2 rows more.

**Next row (RS)** K1, M1, K to last st, M1, K1. 11 (13: 15) sts.

**Next row** As row 3. 13 (15: 17) sts.

Work 6 (8: 10) rows, ending with RS facing for next row.

**Next row (RS)** K1, skp, K to last 3 sts, K2tog, K1.

**Next row** P1, P2tog, P to last 3 sts, P2tog tbl, P1.

Rep last 2 rows once more.

Bind off rem 5 (7: 9) sts.

## Heels (both alike)

With RS facing, using size 7 (4.5mm) needles and CC, starting and ending at markers along row-end edges of one Sole, pick up and knit 9 (10: 11) sts down row-end edge to cast-on edge, 3 (5: 7) sts from cast-on edge, then 9 (10: 11) sts up other row-end edge. 21 (25: 29) sts.

**Rib row 1 (WS)** K1, *P1, K1, rep from * to end.

**Rib row 2** P1, *K1, P1, rep from * to end.

These 2 rows form rib.

Work in rib for 4 (6: 8) rows more, ending with WS facing for next row.

Inc 1 st at each end of next 4 rows, taking inc sts into rib. 29 (33: 37) sts.

Place a marker at each end of last row.

Work in rib for 5 (7: 9) rows more, ending with RS facing for next row.

Bind off in rib.

Work Heel onto second Sole in same way.

### Uppers (both alike)

With RS facing, using size 7 (4.5mm) needles and MC, starting and ending at pick-up row of one Heel, pick up and knit 10 (12: 14) sts up first row-end edge to marker, then 10 (12: 14) sts down other row-end edge from marker. 20 (24: 28) sts.

**Row 1 (WS)** [K1, P1] 7 (8: 9) times and turn.

**Row 2** [P1, K1] 4 times and turn.

**Row 3** [K1, P1] 5 times and turn.

**Row 4** [P1, K1] 6 times and turn.

**Row 5** [K1, P1] 7 times and turn.

**Row 6** [P1, K1] 8 times and turn.

**Row 7** [K1, P1] to end.

Last 7 rows set seed st.

Work in seed st as set for 6 (8: 10) rows more, ending with RS facing for next row.

Join in CC.

Using CC, work in garter st for 2 rows.

Break off CC and cont using MC only.

**Next row (RS)** Knit.

Work in seed st for 3 rows, ending with RS facing for next row.

Dec 1 st at each end of next 8 (9: 10) rows. 4 (6: 8) sts.

Bind off in seed st.

Work Upper onto second Heel in same way.

### Finishing

Do NOT press.

Sew Upper to Sole around front of foot.

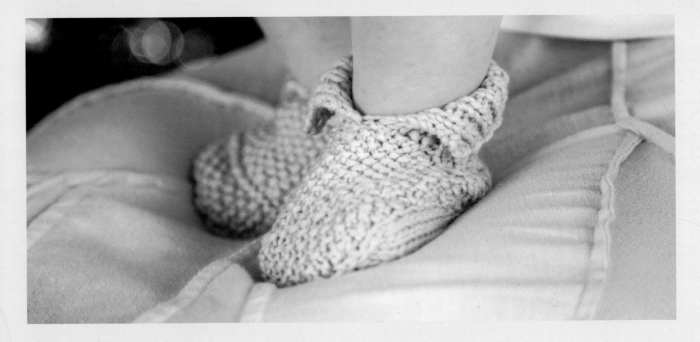

# teddy suit

● ● ● ● ● ● ● ● ●

This is the garment to knit for a real wow factor. Who could resist a baby in this little teddy suit, which is as practical as it is pretty. It will keep baby warm from head to toe, with its hooded and eared hat, and cozy mittens and feet. Intermediate and experienced knitters will enjoy the challenge, too!

Knitted here in blue, the suit would also look great (and even more Teddy-like) in soft beige or, for a girl, in pale mauve.

The yarn is the soft but resilient Rowan *Calmer*.

## To fit age, approximately

| | | | |
|---|---|---|---|
| 0–3 | 3–6 | 6–9 | months |

## Finished measurements

**AROUND CHEST**

| | | | |
|---|---|---|---|
| 20¾ | 22 | 23¼ | in |
| 53 | 56 | 59 | cm |

**LENGTH FROM SHOULDER**

| | | | |
|---|---|---|---|
| 17¼ | 19 | 20½ | in |
| 44 | 48 | 52 | cm |

**SLEEVE SEAM**

| | | | |
|---|---|---|---|
| 5½ | 6¼ | 7 | in |
| 14 | 16 | 18 | cm |

## Yarns

4 (5: 6) x 50g/1¾oz balls of Rowan Calmer in **MC** (*Calmer 463*) and 1 ball in **CC** (Drift 460)

## Needles

Pair of size 7 (4.5mm) knitting needles
Pair of size 8 (5mm) knitting needles

## Extras

12in/30cm zipper

## Gauge

21 sts and 30 rows to 4in/10cm measured over st st using size 8 (5mm) needles *or size to obtain correct gauge.*

## Abbreviations

See page 117.

## Body

### LEFT LEG

Using size 7 (4.5mm) needles and MC, cast on 39 (43: 47) sts.
**Row 1 (RS)** K1, *P1, K1, rep from * to end.

**Row 2** P1, *K1, P1, rep from * to end.
These 2 rows form rib.
Work in rib for 1 (1½: 2)in/3 (4: 5)cm, ending with WS facing for next row.
**Row 6 (WS)** Rib 3 (5: 1), M1, *rib 3 (3: 4), M1, rep from * to last 3 (5: 2) sts, rib to end. 51 (55: 59) sts.
Change to size 8 (5mm) needles.
Work in patt as foll:
**Row 1 (RS)** K3, *P1, K3, rep from * to end.
**Row 2** Purl.
**Row 3** K1, *P1, K3, rep from * to last 2 sts, P1, K1.
**Row 4** Purl.
These 4 rows form patt.
Work in patt, shaping leg by inc 1 st at each end of next row and every foll alt row until there are 75 (83: 91) sts, taking inc sts into patt.
Work even until Leg measures 4¾ (6: 7)in/12 (15: 18)cm, ending with RS facing for next row.

### SHAPE CROTCH

Keeping patt correct, bind off 3 (4: 5) sts at beg of next 2 rows. 69 (75: 81) sts.
Dec 1 st at each end of next row and foll 3 (4: 5) alt rows. 61 (65: 69) sts.
Work 1 row, ending with RS facing for next row.**
Break off yarn and leave sts on a holder.

### RIGHT LEG

Work as given for Left Leg to **.

### JOIN LEGS

With RS facing, work across first 60 (64: 68) sts of Right Leg, K tog last st of Right Leg with first st of Left Leg, then work across rem 60 (64: 68) sts of Left Leg. 121 (129: 137) sts.
Work even until body measures 2¾in/7cm from crotch bound-off edge, ending with RS facing for next row.

### START FRONT OPENING

Place a marker at each end of last row to denote base of front opening.

## CHART A

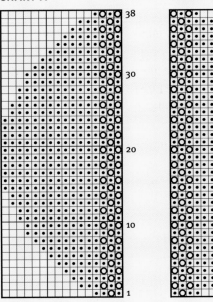

## CHART B

## KEY

☐ using MC, patt
▣ using CC, K on RS, P on WS
◉ using CC, P on RS, K on WS

**Next row (RS)** K1, P1, K1, patt to last 3 sts, K1, P1, K1.
**Next row** K1, P1, K1, patt to last 3 sts, K1, P1, K1.

### PLACE TUMMY PATCH

Join in CC and, twisting yarns together where they meet to avoid holes forming, place charts for tummy patch as foll:
**Next row (RS)** Work first 16 sts as row 1 of chart A, patt to last 16 sts, work last 16 sts as row 1 of chart B.
**Next row** Work first 16 sts as row 2 of chart B, patt to last 16 sts, work last 16 sts as row 2 of chart A.
These 2 rows set position of charts.
Work as set until all 38 rows of charts have been completed, ending with RS facing for next row.
Break off CC and cont using MC only.
**Next row (RS)** K1, P1, K1, patt to last 3 sts, K1, P1, K1.

**Next row** K1, P1, K1, patt to last 3 sts, K1, P1, K1.
These 2 rows set the sts—front opening edge 3 sts now in seed st with all other sts still in patt.
Work even until body measures 5in/13cm from base of front opening, ending with WS facing for next row.

### SHAPE LEFT FRONT

**Next row (WS)** Patt 30 (33: 34) sts and turn, leaving rem sts on a holder.
Work on this set of 30 (33: 34) sts only for left front.
Work even until left front measures 3½ (4: 4¼)in/ 9 (10: 11)cm from dividing row, ending with RS facing for next row.

### SHAPE NECK

**Next row (RS)** Patt to last 9 (10: 11) sts and turn, leaving rem sts on another holder. 21 (23: 23) sts.
Dec 1 st at neck edge of next 5 (6: 5) rows. 16 (17: 18) sts.
Work even until left front measures 4¾ (5: 5½)in/12 (13: 14)cm from dividing row, ending with RS facing for next row.

### SHAPE SHOULDER

Bind off 8 (9: 9) sts at beg of next row.
Work 1 row.
Bind off rem 8 (8: 9) sts.

### SHAPE BACK

With WS facing, rejoin yarn to sts on first holder, patt 61 (63: 69) sts and turn, leaving rem sts on a holder.
Work on this set of 61 (63: 69) sts only for back.
Work even until back measures 4¾ (5: 5½)in/12 (13: 14)cm from dividing row, ending with RS facing for next row.

### SHAPE SHOULDERS

Bind off 8 (9: 9) sts at beg of next 2 rows, then 8 (8: 9) sts at beg of foll 2 rows.
Break off yarn and leave rem 29 (29: 33) sts on another holder.

### SHAPE RIGHT FRONT

With WS facing, rejoin yarn to sts on first holder, patt to end.
Work on this set of 30 (33: 34) sts only for right front.
Complete to match left front, reversing shapings.

## Sleeves

Using size 7 (4.5mm) needles and MC, cast on 29 (33: 37) sts.

Work in rib as given for Left Leg for 1½in/4cm, ending with WS facing for next row.

**Next row (WS)** Rib 2 (1: 3), M1, *rib 5 (6: 6), M1, rep from * to last 2 (2: 4) sts, rib to end. 35 (39: 43) sts.

Change to size 8 (5mm) needles.

Starting with patt row 1, work in patt as given for Left Leg, shaping sides by inc 1 st at each end of 5th row and every foll 3rd row until there are 51 (59: 67) sts, taking inc sts into patt.

Work even until Sleeve measures 5½ (6¼: 7)in/14 (16: 18)cm, ending with RS facing for next row.

Bind off.

## Finishing

Press lightly on WS following instructions on yarn label.

Sew shoulder seams.

### HOOD

With RS facing, using size 7 (4.5mm) needles and MC, slip 9 (10: 11) sts from right front holder onto right needle, pick up and knit 13 (14: 13) sts up right side of neck, K across 29 (29: 33) sts on back holder, pick up and knit 13 (14: 13) sts down left side of neck, then patt across 9 (10: 11) sts on left front holder. 73 (77: 81) sts.

**Row 1 (WS)** K1, *P1, K1, rep from * to end.

**Row 2** K1, P1, K2, *P1, K1, rep from * to last 3 sts, K1, P1, K1.

These 2 rows set the sts—front opening edge 3 sts still in seed st with all other sts in rib.

Work as set for 3 rows more, ending with RS

facing for next row.

**Row 6 (RS)** Patt 5 sts and slip these sts onto a holder, rib 4 (6: 8), M1, *rib 5, M1, rep from * to last 9 (11: 13) sts, rib 4 (6: 8) and turn, leaving rem 5 sts on another holder. 75 (79: 83) sts.

Change to size 8 (5mm) needles.

Starting with patt row 2, work in patt as given for Left Leg until Hood measures 4¾ (5½: 6¼)in/12 (14: 16)cm, ending with RS facing for next row.

### SHAPE TOP

**Row 1 (RS)** Patt 50 (52: 54) sts and turn.

**Row 2** Sl 1, patt 23 sts, P2tog and turn.

**Row 3** Sl 1, patt 23 sts, skp and turn.

Rep rows 2 and 3, 24 (26: 28) times more.

Break off yarn and leave rem 25 sts on a holder.

### HOOD BORDER

With RS facing, using size 7 (4.5mm) needles and MC, slip 5 sts from right front holder onto right needle, pick up and knit 25 (29: 33) sts up right side of hood, K across 25 sts on hood holder, pick up and knit 25 (29: 33) sts down left side of hood, then patt across 5 sts on left front holder. 85 (93: 101) sts.

**Row 1 (WS)** K1, *P1, K1, rep from * to end.

Rep this row 5 times more.

Bind off in seed st.

Sew back crotch seam, from bound-off edge to where sections are joined. Sew front crotch seam, from bound-off edge to base of front opening. Sew sleeve seams. Sew Sleeves into armholes, matching top of sleeve seam to center of bound-off sts at underarm and center of sleeve bound-off edge to shoulder seam. Sew zipper into front opening.

### OUTER EARS (make 2)

Using size 8 (5mm) needles and MC, cast on 15 sts.

**Row 1 (RS)** K1, *P1, K1, rep from * to end.

**Row 2** As row 1.

These 2 rows form seed st.

Work in seed st for 7 rows more, ending with WS facing for next row.

Dec 1 st at each end of next row and foll 3 alt rows, ending with RS facing for next row.

Bind off rem 7 sts in seed st.

### INNER EARS (make 2)

Work as given for Outer Ears but using CC.

Sew Inner and Outer Ears together, leaving cast-on edges open. Make a pleat in cast-on edges, then sew Ears to Hood as in photograph.

### LEFT MITT

Using size 8 (5mm) needles and MC, cast on 27 (31: 35) sts.

Work in seed st as given for Outer Ear for 8 (10: 12) rows, ending with RS facing for next row.**

### SHAPE PALM PATCH

Bind off 13 (15: 17) sts at beg of next row. 14 (16: 18) sts.

Work 1 row.

Keeping seed st correct as set, join in CC and work as foll:

**Row 3 (RS)** Using CC cast on and seed st 13 (15: 17) sts, using MC seed st to end. 27 (31: 35) sts.

**Row 4** Using MC seed st 14 (16: 18) sts, using CC seed st 13 (15: 17) sts.

**Row 5** Using CC seed st 13 (15: 17) sts, using MC seed st to end.

**Rows 6 to 9** As rows 4 and 5, twice.

**Row 10** As row 4.

Break off CC and cont using MC only.

**Row 11 (RS)** K13 (15: 17), seed st to end.

***Work in seed st for 1 row, ending with RS facing for next row.

### SHAPE TOP

**Row 1 (RS)** Work 2 tog, seed st 10 (12: 14) sts, work 3 tog, seed st to last 2 sts, work 2 tog. 23 (27: 31) sts.

Work 1 row.

**Row 3** Work 2 tog, seed st 8 (10: 12) sts, work 3 tog, seed st

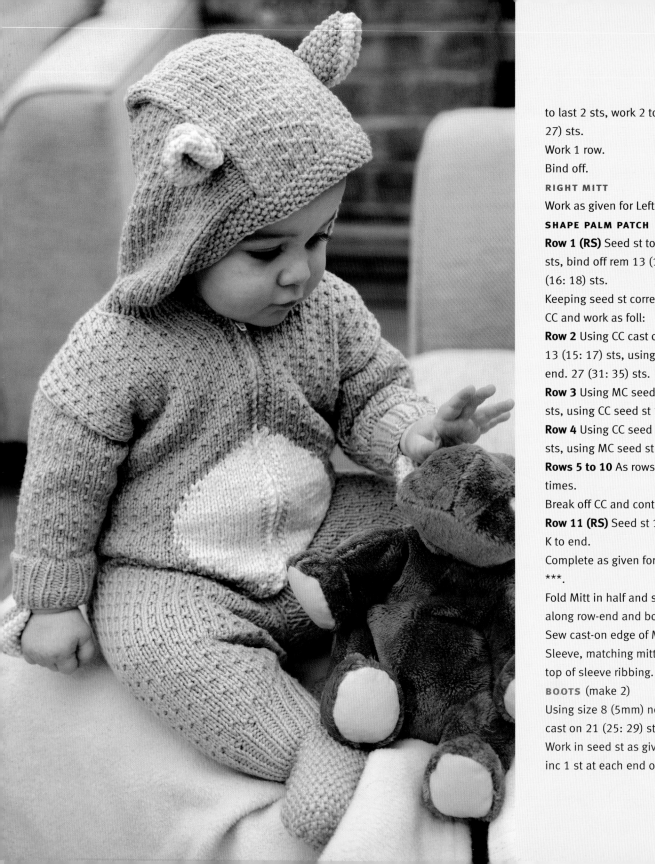

to last 2 sts, work 2 tog. 19 (23: 27) sts.

Work 1 row.

Bind off.

**RIGHT MITT**

Work as given for Left Mitt to **.

**SHAPE PALM PATCH**

**Row 1 (RS)** Seed st to last 13 (15: 17) sts, bind off rem 13 (15: 17) sts. 14 (16: 18) sts.

Keeping seed st correct as set, join in CC and work as foll:

**Row 2** Using CC cast on and seed st 13 (15: 17) sts, using MC seed st to end. 27 (31: 35) sts.

**Row 3** Using MC seed st 14 (16: 18) sts, using CC seed st 13 (15: 17) sts.

**Row 4** Using CC seed st 13 (15: 17) sts, using MC seed st to end.

**Rows 5 to 10** As rows 3 and 4, 3 times.

Break off CC and cont using MC only.

**Row 11 (RS)** Seed st 14 (16: 18) sts, K to end.

Complete as given for Left Mitt from ***.

Fold Mitt in half and sew together along row-end and bound-off edges. Sew cast-on edge of Mitt inside Sleeve, matching mitt cast-on edge to top of sleeve ribbing.

**BOOTS** (make 2)

Using size 8 (5mm) needles and MC, cast on 21 (25: 29) sts.

Work in seed st as given for Outer Ear, inc 1 st at each end of 2nd row and

foll 4 (5: 6) alt rows, ending with RS facing for next row. 31 (37: 43) sts.
Work 1 row.

Dec 1 st at each end of next row and foll 4 (5: 6) alt rows, ending with RS facing for next row. 21 (25: 29) sts.

**SHAPE HEEL**

Cast on 5 (6: 7) sts at beg of next row. 26 (31: 36) sts.

Inc 1 st at end of 2nd row and foll 4 (5: 6) alt rows. 31 (37: 43) sts.
Work 2 rows, ending with RS facing for next row.

**Next row (RS)** Bind off 14 (16: 18) sts, seed st to last st, inc in last st. 18 (22: 26) sts.

Work 10 (14: 18) rows, ending with WS facing for next row.

Dec 1 st at beg of next row. 17 (21: 25) sts.

Cast on 14 (16: 18) sts at beg of next row. 31 (37: 43) sts.

Dec 1 st at beg of next row and foll 4 (5: 6) alt rows. 26 (31: 36) sts.
Work 1 row, ending with RS facing for next row.

Bind off in seed st.

Sew heel seam, then sew upper to sole, easing in slight fullness. Sew top of Boot to cast-on edge of Legs as in photograph.

# cable and lace wrap cardigan

· · · · · · · · · ·

Ideal for wearing on a cool day over a summer dress, this great girly cardigan is also versatile enough to wear with casual jeans.

Make it in any sugar-almond pastel colorway for maximum effect. It is wonderfully adjustable, too, so no need to worry about the fit. If you like to try your hand at new stitches, you will love working the cable and lacy panels around the base of the cardigan and the sleeves.

The deliciously soft Rowan *Cashsoft Baby DK* used here is a really luxurious yarn but it still goes in the washing machine without a hitch.

**To fit age, approximately**

| 6–12 | 12–18 | 18–24 | months |
|------|-------|-------|--------|

**Finished measurements**

**AROUND CHEST**

| 23½ | 25½ | 27½ | in |
|-----|-----|-----|-----|
| 60 | 65 | 70 | cm |

**LENGTH FROM SHOULDER**

| 12½ | 14 | 15¾ | in |
|-----|-----|-----|-----|
| 32 | 36 | 40 | cm |

**SLEEVE SEAM**

| 6¾ | 7¾ | 8¾ | in |
|-----|-----|-----|-----|
| 17 | 20 | 22 | cm |

## Yarns

5 (5: 6) x 50g/1¾oz balls of Rowan *RYC Cashsoft Baby DK* in Cloud 805

## Needles

Pair of size 3 (3.25mm) knitting needles
Pair of size 6 (4mm) knitting needles
Cable needle

## Extras

1 button

## Gauge

22 sts and 30 rows to 4in/10cm measured over st st using size 6 (4mm) needles *or size to obtain correct gauge.*

## Abbreviations

**C4B** = slip next 2 sts onto cable needle and leave at back of work, K2, then K2 from cable needle; **C4F** = slip next 2 sts onto cable needle and leave at front of work, K2, then K2 from cable needle; **C5B** = slip next 2 sts onto cable needle and leave at back of work, K3, then K2 from cable needle.
See also page 117.

**Back and fronts** (worked in one piece to armholes)
Using size 3 (3.25mm) needles, cast on 176 (193: 210) sts.
Work in garter st (K every row) for 3 rows, ending with RS facing for next row.
Change to size 6 (4mm) needles.
Work in cable and lace patt as foll:
**Row 1 (RS)** K3, *K4, K2tog, K3, yo, K8, rep from * to last 3 sts, K3.
**Row 2** K3, P to last 3 sts, K3.
**Row 3** K3, *K3, K2tog, K3, yo, K1, yo, K3, skp, K3, rep from * to last 3 sts, K3.
**Row 4** As row 2.
**Row 5** K3, *K2, K2tog, [K3, yo] twice, K3, skp, K2, rep from * to last 3 sts, K3.
**Row 6** As row 2.
**Row 7** K3, *K1, K2tog, K3, yo, K5, yo, K3, skp, K1, rep from * to last 3 sts, K3.
**Row 8** As row 2.
**Row 9** K3, *K2tog, K3, yo, P1, C5B, P1, yo, K3, skp, rep from * to last 3 sts, K3.
**Row 10** K3, *P4, K2, P5, K2, P4, rep from * to last 3 sts, K3.
**Row 11** K3, *K4, P2, K5, P2, K4; rep from * to last 3 sts, K3.
**Row 12** As row 10.
**Row 13** K3, *C4B, P2, K5, P2, C4F, rep from * to last 3 sts, K3.
**Row 14** As row 10.
**Rows 15 to 18** As rows 11 to 14.
**Rows 19 and 20** As rows 11 and 12.
**Row 21** K3, *C4B, K2tog, K3, yo, K4, C4F, rep from * to last 3 sts, K3.
**Row 22** As row 2.
**Rows 23 to 42** As rows 1 to 20.
**Row 43** K3, *C4B, K9, C4F, rep from * to last 3 sts, K3.
**Row 44** K3, P21 (11: 11), P2tog, [P40 (25: 18), P2tog] 3 (6: 9) times, P to last 3 sts, K3. 172 (186: 200) sts.
These 44 rows complete cable and lace border.

**Next row (RS)** Knit.

**Next row** K3, P to last 3 sts, K3.

Rep last 2 rows (2: 3) times more, ending with RS facing for next row.

**ALL SIZES**

Starting with a K row, work in st st as foll:

### SHAPE FRONT SLOPES

**Next row (RS)** K3 and slip these 3 sts onto a holder, K3, skp, K to last 8 sts, K2tog, K3 and turn, leaving last 3 sts on another holder. 164 (178: 192) sts.

**Next row** P3, P2tog, P to last 5 sts, P2tog tbl, P3.

**Next row** K3, skp, K to last 5 sts, K2tog, K3.

Working all decreases as set by last 2 rows, dec 1 st at each end of next 15 (17: 19) rows, ending with RS facing for next row. 130 (140: 150) sts.

### DIVIDE FOR BACK AND FRONTS

**Next row (RS)** K3, skp, K25 (27: 29) and slip these 29 (31: 33) sts onto a holder for right front, bind off 4 sts, K until there are 62 (68: 74) sts on right needle and slip these sts onto another holder for back, bind off 4 sts, K to last 5 sts, K2tog, K3.

Work on this last set of 29 (31: 33) sts only for left front.

### SHAPE LEFT FRONT

Working all decreases as set by front slope decreases, dec 1 st at each end of 2nd row and foll 3 alt rows. 21 (23: 25) sts.

Dec 1 st at front slope edge **only** on 2nd row and every foll alt row until 13 (14: 15) sts rem.

Work even until armhole measures 4¼ (4¾: 5)in/11 (12: 13)cm, ending with RS facing for next row.

### SHAPE SHOULDER

Bind off.

### SHAPE BACK

With WS facing, rejoin yarn to 62 (68: 74) sts on back holder, P to end.

Working all decreases as set by front slope decreases, dec

1 st at each end of next row and foll 3 alt rows. 54 (60: 66) sts.

Work even until back matches left front to shoulder, ending with RS facing for next row.

### SHAPE SHOULDER

Bind off 13 (14: 15) sts at beg of next 2 rows. 28 (32: 36) sts.

Change to size 3 (3.25mm) needles.

Work in garter st for 4 rows for back neck border, ending with RS facing for next row.

Bind off.

### SHAPE RIGHT FRONT

With WS facing, rejoin yarn to 29 (31: 33) sts on right front holder, P to end.

Complete to match left front, reversing shapings.

## Sleeves

Using size 3 (3.25mm) needles, cast on 53 sts.

Work in garter st for 3 rows, ending with RS facing for next row.

Change to size 6 (4mm) needles.

Work in cable and lace patt as foll:

**Row 1 (RS)** K1, *K4, K2tog, K3, yo, K8, rep from * to last st, K1.

**Row 2** Purl.

**Row 3** K1, *K3, K2tog, K3, yo, K1, yo, K3, skp, K3, rep from * to last st, K1.

**Row 4** As row 2.

**Row 5** K1, *K2, K2tog, [K3, yo] twice, K3, skp, K2, rep from * to last st, K1.

**Row 6** As row 2.

**Row 7** K1, *K1, K2tog, K3, yo, K5, yo,

K3, skp, K1, rep from * to last st, K1.

**Row 8** As row 2.

**Row 9** K1, *K2tog, K3, yo, P1, C5B, P1, yo, K3, skp, rep from * to last st, K1.

**Row 10** P1, *P4, K2, P5, K2, P4, rep from * to last st, P1.

**Row 11** K1, *K4, P2, K5, P2, K4; rep from * to last st, P1.

**Row 12** As row 10.

**Row 13** K1, *C4B, P2, K5, P2, C4F, rep from * to last st, K1.

**Row 14** As row 10.

**Rows 15 to 18** As rows 11 to 14.

**Rows 19 and 20** As rows 11 and 12.

**Row 21** K1, *C4B, K2tog, K3, yo, K4, C4F, rep from * to last st, K1.

**Row 22** As row 2.

These 22 rows complete cable and lace border.

Starting with a K row, work in st st as foll:

**SIZES 12–18 AND 18–24 MONTHS ONLY**

Inc 1 st at each end of (13th: 9th) row and every foll (12th: 8th) row until there are (57: 61) sts.

**ALL SIZES**

Work even until Sleeve measures 6¾ (7¾: 8¾)in/17 (20: 22)cm, ending with RS facing for next row.

**SHAPE TOP OF SLEEVE**

Bind off 3 sts at beg of next 2 rows. 47 (51: 55) sts.

Working all decreases in same way as for front slope decreases, dec 1 st at each end of next row and foll 3 alt rows.

Work 1 row, ending with RS facing for next row.

Bind off rem 39 (43: 47) sts.

## Finishing

Press lightly on WS following instructions on yarn label.

Sew both shoulder seams.

**RIGHT FRONT BORDER AND TIE**

With RS facing and using size 3 (3.25mm) needles, cast on 90 sts, K across 3 sts on right front holder, then pick up and knit 52 (56: 60) sts up right front slope. 145 (149: 153) sts.

Work in garter st for 3 rows, ending with RS facing for next row.

Bind off.

**LEFT FRONT BORDER**

With RS facing and using size 3 (3.25mm) needles, pick up and knit 52 (56: 60) sts down left front slope, K across 3 sts on right front holder. 55 (59: 63) sts.

**Row 1 (WS)** Knit.

**Row 2** K to last 4 sts, K2tog, yo (to make a buttonhole), K2.

**Row 3** Knit.

Bind off.

**LEFT TIE**

Using size 3 (3.25mm) needles, cast on 90 sts.

Work in garter st for 3 rows.

Bind off.

Sew sleeve seams. Sew Sleeves to armholes. Sew row-end edges of front Borders to back neck border. Sew Left Tie to outside of left front level with start of front slope shaping and directly below armhole. Sew button to inside of right front to correspond with buttonhole.

# ruffled dress

• • • • • • • • •

This is the perfect dress for a little girl with its dainty ruffles around the skirt and at the back. A pinafore dress is always useful, too, as you can change the look with the tops and blouses your child wears underneath. The button opening at the back makes it easy to get on and off.

This design is knitted in Rowan *Wool Cotton*, which is a great yarn for year-round wear, and, like all the yarns used in this book, it machine washes beautifully.

The dress has some very nice detailing on the seams and a particularly pretty and comfortable softly rolled, low round neckline.

Guaranteed to be a classic!

## To fit age, approximately

| 3–6 | 9–12 | 12–18 | 18–24 | months |
|---|---|---|---|---|

### Finished measurements

**AROUND CHEST**

| 19 | 20½ | 22 | 24½ | in |
|---|---|---|---|---|
| 48 | 52 | 56 | 62 | cm |

**LENGTH FROM SHOULDER**

| 14¼ | 16¼ | 18½ | 21¼ | in |
|---|---|---|---|---|
| 36 | 41 | 47 | 54 | cm |

## Yarns

4 (5: 5: 6) x 50g/1¾oz balls of Rowan *Wool Cotton* in Tender 951

## Needles

Pair of size 3 (3.25mm) knitting needles
Pair of size 6 (4mm) knitting needles
Size 3 (3.25mm) circular knitting needle
Size 6 (4mm) circular knitting needle

## Extras

4 buttons

## Gauge

22 sts and 30 rows to 4in/10cm measured over st st using size 6 (4mm) needles *or size to obtain correct gauge*.

## Abbreviations

See page 117.

## Back

### TOP RUFFLE

Using size 3 (3.25mm) needles, cast on 39 sts.
**Knit 1 row, ending with RS facing for next row.
Change to size 6 (4mm) needles.
Work ruffle as foll:

**Row 1 (RS)** P3, *K9, P3, rep from * to end.
**Row 2** K3, *P9, K3, rep from * to end.
**Row 3** P3, *skp, K5, K2tog, P3, rep from * to end.
**Row 4** K3, *P7, K3, rep from * to end.
**Row 5** P3, *skp, K3, K2tog, P3, rep from * to end.
**Row 6** K3, *P5, K3, rep from * to end.
**Row 7** P3, *skp, K1, K2tog, P3, rep from * to end.
**Row 8** K3, *P3, K3, rep from * to end.
**Row 9** P3, *sk2p, P3, rep from * to end.** 15 sts.
Break off yarn and leave sts on a holder.

### MIDDLE RUFFLE

Using size 3 (3.25mm) needles, cast on 63 sts.
Work as given for Top Ruffle from ** to **. 23 sts.
Break off yarn and leave sts on another holder.

### MAIN SECTION

Using size 3 (3.25mm) circular needle, cast on 207 (231: 255: 279) sts.
Work as given for Top Ruffle from ** to **, changing to size 6 (4mm) circular needle after first row. 71 (79: 87: 95) sts.
Change to size 3 (3.25mm) needles.
Work in garter st (K every row) for 3 rows, ending with RS facing for next row.
Change to size 6 (4mm) needles.

### SHAPE RUFFLE PANEL

Counting in from both ends of last row, place a marker on 19th (23rd: 27th: 31st) st in from each end of row.
**Row 1 (RS)** K2, P1, K to marked st, M1P, K marked st, skp, P to within 2 sts of next marked st, K2tog, K marked st, M1P, K to last 3 sts, P1, K2.
**Row 2** P to marked st, P marked st, P1, K to within 1 st of next marked st, P1, P marked st, P to end.
**Rows 3 to 6** As rows 1 and 2, twice.
**Row 7** As row 1.
**Row 8** P24 (28: 32: 36), with WS of Middle Ruffle against RS of Back K tog first st of Ruffle with next st of Back, [K tog next st of Ruffle with next st of Back] 22 times, P to end.

**Rows 9 to 14** As rows 1 and 2, 3 times.

**Row 15** As row 1.

**Row 16** P28 (32: 36: 40), with WS of Top Ruffle against RS of Back K tog first st of Ruffle with next st of Back, [K tog next st of Ruffle with next st of Back] 14 times, P to end.

**Row 17** As row 1.

**Row 18** Purl.

**Row 19** K2, P1, K24 (28: 32: 36), P1, K3, P1, K7, P1, K3, P1, K to last 3 sts, P1, K2.

**Row 20** Purl.

These 20 rows complete ruffle panel.

Cont in main patt as foll:

**Row 1 (RS)** K2, P1, K30 (34: 38: 42), P1, K3, P1, K to last 3 sts, P1, K2.

**Row 2** Purl.

These 2 rows form main patt.

### ***SHAPE SKIRT

Place a marker at each side of center 13 sts.

**Next row (dec row) (RS)** Patt 7 sts, skp, K to within 2 sts of marker, K2tog, slip marker onto right needle, patt 13 sts, slip marker onto right needle, skp, K to last 9 sts, K2tog, patt to end.

Work 9 (9: 11: 13) rows, ending with RS facing for next row.

Rep last 10 (10: 12: 14) rows 2 (3: 3: 4) times more, then first of these rows (the dec row) again. 55 (59: 67: 71) sts.

Work 3 (6: 9: 6) rows.

### SIZES 3–6 AND 12–18 MONTHS ONLY

**Next row (RS)** Patt 7 sts, skp, patt to last 9 sts, K2tog, patt to end. 53 (65) sts.

### ALL SIZES

Change to size 3 (3.25mm) needles.

Work in garter st for 4 rows, ending with RS facing for next row.

Change to size 6 (4mm) needles.***

### DIVIDE FOR BACK OPENING

**Next row (RS)** Patt 25 (28: 31: 34) sts and turn, leaving rem

sts on a holder.

Work each side of neck separately.

**Next row (WS)** Cast on and K 3 sts, P to end. 28 (31: 34: 37) sts.

**Next row** Patt to last 3 sts, K3.

**Next row** K3, P to end.

These 2 rows set the sts—back opening edge 3 sts in garter st with all other sts still in patt.

Keeping sts correct as now set, work even until Back measures 10¼ (11¾: 13¾: 16)in/26 (30: 35: 41)cm, ending with RS facing for next row.

### SHAPE ARMHOLE

Keeping sts correct, bind off 6 sts at beg of next row, then 4 sts at beg of foll alt row. 18 (21: 24: 27) sts.

Work 1 row, ending with RS facing for next row.

**Next row (RS)** K2, P2tog, K to end.

**Next row** K3, P to end.

Rep last 2 rows 2 (3: 3: 4) times more. 15 (17: 20: 22) sts.

**Next row (RS)** K2, P1, K to end.

**Next row** K3, P to end.

Rep last 2 rows until armhole measures 2¾ (3: 3: 3½)in/ 7 (8: 8: 9)cm, ending with RS facing for next row.

### SHAPE NECK

**Next row (RS)** Patt to last 6 (7: 8: 9) sts and turn, leaving rem 6 (7: 8: 9) sts on a holder. 9 (10: 12: 13) sts.

Dec 1 st at neck edge of next 4 rows. 5 (6: 8: 9) sts.

Work even until armhole measures 4 (4¼: 4¾: 5)in/10 (11: 12: 13)cm, ending with RS facing for next row.

### SHAPE SHOULDER

Bind off.

Mark positions for 4 buttons along right back opening edge—first to come 1⅛in/3cm up from base of opening, last to come ⅜in/1cm below neck shaping and rem 2 buttons evenly spaced between.

With RS facing, rejoin yarn to rem sts, patt to end.

**Next row (WS)** Patt to last 3 sts, K3. 28 (31: 34: 37) sts.

**Next row** K3, patt to end.

These 2 rows set the sts—back opening edge 3 sts in garter st with all other sts still in patt.

Complete to match first side, reversing shapings, **and at the same time** make 4 buttonholes to correspond with positions marked for buttons as foll:

**Buttonhole row (RS)** K1, K2tog, yo, patt to end.

### Front

Using size 3 (3.25mm) circular needle, cast on 207 (231: 255: 279) sts.

Work as given for Top Ruffle of Back from ** to **, changing to size 6 (4mm) circular needle after first row. 71 (79: 87: 95) sts.

Change to size 3 (3.25mm) needles.

Work in garter st for 3 rows, ending with RS facing for next row.

Change to size 6 (4mm) needles.

Cont in patt as foll:

**Row 1 (RS)** K2, P1, K30 (34: 38: 42), P1, K3, P1, K to last 3 sts, P1, K2.

**Row 2** Purl.

These 2 rows form main patt.

Work 20 rows, ending with RS facing for next row.

Work as given for Back from *** to ***.

Work even in patt until Front matches Back to start of armhole shaping, ending with RS facing for next row.

#### SHAPE ARMHOLES

Keeping patt correct, bind off 6 sts at beg of next 2 rows, then 4 sts at beg of foll 2 rows. 33 (39: 45: 51) sts.

**Next row (RS)** K2, P2tog, patt to last 4 sts, P2tog, K2.

**Next row** Purl.

Rep last 2 rows 2 (3: 3: 4) times more. 27 (31: 37: 41) sts.

**Next row (RS)** K2, P1, patt to last 3 sts, P1, K2.

**Next row** Purl.

Rep last 2 rows until armhole measures 2¼in/5.5cm, ending

with RS facing for next row.

#### SHAPE NECK

**Next row (RS)** Patt 10 (11: 13: 14) sts and turn, leaving rem sts on a holder.

Work each side of neck separately.

Dec 1 st at neck edge of next row and foll 4 alt rows. 5 (6: 8: 9) sts.

Work even until Front matches Back to shoulder bind-off, ending with RS facing for next row.

#### SHAPE SHOULDER

Bind off.

With RS facing, slip center 7 (9: 11: 13) sts onto a holder, rejoin yarn to rem sts, patt to end.

Complete to match first side, reversing shapings.

### Finishing

Press lightly on WS following instructions on yarn label.

Sew both shoulder seams.

#### NECKBAND

With RS facing and using size 3 (3.25mm) needles, slip 6 (7: 8: 9) sts from left back holder onto right needle, rejoin yarn and pick up and knit 7 sts up left side of back neck, and 15 (15: 16: 16) sts down left side of front neck, K across 7 (9: 11: 13) sts on front holder, pick up and knit 15 (15: 16: 16) sts up right side of front neck, and 7 sts down right side of back neck, then K across 6 (7: 8: 9) sts on right back holder. 63 (67: 73: 77) sts.

Starting with a P row, work in st st for 4 rows, ending with WS facing for next row.

Bind off purlwise.

#### ARMHOLE BORDERS (both alike)

With RS facing and using size 3 (3.25mm) needles, pick up and knit 54 (60: 66: 72) sts evenly all around armhole edge.

Starting with a P row, work in st st for 4 rows, ending with WS facing for next row.

Bind off purlwise.

Sew side and Armhole Border seams, reversing seams for Armhole Borders.

**POCKETS** (make 2)

Using size 6 (4mm) needles, cast on 16 (16: 18: 18) sts.

Knit 1 row, ending with RS facing for next row.

**Next row (RS)** Knit.

**Next row** P2, K1, P to last 3 sts, K1, P2.

Rep last 2 rows 8 times more.

**Next row (RS)** K3, skp, K to last 5 sts, K2tog, K3.

**Next row** P2, K1, P to last 3 sts, K1, P2.

Rep last 2 rows twice more.

Bind off rem 10 (10: 12: 12) sts.

Using photograph as a guide, sew Pockets onto Back. Sew cast-on sts at base of back opening in place on WS. Sew on buttons. Neatly sew down row-end edges of Top and Middle Ruffles as in photograph.

# picot-edged sweater

· · · · · · · · · ·

This design has a simple loose and quite long tunic shape, with really smart finishing details in the double picot and garter stitch edging at the hem and the single picot edging on the sleeves and neckline. The wide neckline, finished with a picot-edged tie, has button-up fastening at the back and fits easily over a baby or child's head.

Knitted in soft and luxurious Rowan *Cashsoft Baby DK*, the sweater holds its shape well and is comfortable to wear. It goes equally well over a little skirt or trousers.

## To fit age, approximately

| 6–12 | 12–18 | 18–24 | months |
|------|-------|-------|--------|

### Finished measurements

#### AROUND CHEST

| | | | |
|------|-------|-------|-----|
| 23½ | 25½ | 28 | in |
| 60 | 65 | 71 | cm |

#### LENGTH FROM SHOULDER

| | | | |
|------|-------|-------|-----|
| 12½ | 14 | 15¾ | in |
| 32 | 36 | 40 | cm |

#### SLEEVE SEAM

| | | | |
|------|-------|-------|-----|
| 6½ | 7¾ | 8½ | in |
| 17 | 20 | 22 | cm |

## Yarns

4 (5: 6) x 50g/1¾oz balls of Rowan *RYC Cashsoft Baby DK* in Chicory 804

## Needles

Pair of size 3 (3.25mm) knitting needles
Pair of size 6 (4mm) knitting needles
Size 3 (3.25mm) circular knitting needle

## Extras

1 small button

## Gauge

22 sts and 30 rows to 4in/10cm measured over st st using size 6 (4mm) needles *or size to obtain correct gauge.*

## Abbreviations

See page 117.

## Edgings (make 2)

Using size 3 (3.25mm) needles, cast on 72 (80: 88) sts.
Work in garter st (K every row) for 6 rows, ending with RS facing for next row.

Break off yarn and leave sts on a holder.

### PICOTS

With RS facing and using size 3 (3.25mm) needles, pick up and knit 72 (80: 88) sts along cast-on edge of Edging.
Work picot bind-off as foll: bind off 3 (4: 3) sts (one st on right needle), *slip st on right needle back onto left needle, cast on 2 sts onto left needle, bind off 5 sts (one st on right needle), rep from * to end, ending last rep with bind off 5 (6: 6) sts.

## Back

Using size 3 (3.25mm) needles, cast on 76 (84: 92) sts.
Work in garter st for 6 rows, ending with RS facing for next row.
Change to size 6 (4mm) needles.
Starting with a K row, work in st st for 4 rows, ending with RS facing for next row.
**Next row (RS)** K6, skp, K to last 8 sts, K2tog, K6. 74 (82: 90) sts.
Working all side seam decreases as set by last row, cont as foll:
Work 7 rows, ending with RS facing for next row.

### JOIN EDGING

**Next row (RS)** K1, holding WS of Edging against RS of Back, K tog first st of Edging with first st of Back, *K tog next st of Edging with next st of Back, rep from * to last st, K1.
Dec 1 st at each end of 2nd row and every foll 10th row until 66 (72: 78) sts rem.
Work even until Back measures 8¼ (9½: 10½)in/21 (24: 27)cm, ending with RS facing for next row.

### SHAPE ARMHOLES

Bind off 3 sts at beg of next 2 rows. 60 (66: 72) sts.
**Next row (RS)** K3, skp, K to last 5 sts, K2tog, K3.
Working all armhole decreases as set by last row, dec 1 st at each end of 2nd row and foll 2 alt rows. 52 (58: 64) sts.
Work even until armhole measures 2¼ (2¾: 3)in/6 (7: 8)cm, ending with RS facing for next row.

## DIVIDE FOR BACK OPENING

**Next row (RS)** K26 (29: 32) and turn, leaving rem sts on a holder.

Work each side of neck separately.

**Next row (WS)** K2, P to end.

**Next row** Knit.

These 2 rows set the sts—back opening edge 2 sts in garter st with all other sts still in st st. Keeping sts correct as now set, work even until armhole measures 4¼ (4¾: 5)in/11 (12: 13)cm, ending with RS facing for next row.

### SHAPE SHOULDER

Bind off 13 (14: 15) sts at beg of next row.

Break off yarn and leave rem 13 (15: 17) sts on a holder.

With RS facing, rejoin yarn to rem sts, K to end.

**Next row (WS)** P to last 2 sts, K2.

**Next row** Knit.

These 2 rows set the sts—back opening edge 2 sts in garter st with all other sts still in st st.

Complete to match first side, reversing shapings.

## Front

Work as given for Back to start of back opening, ending with RS facing for next row.

### SHAPE FRONT NECK

**Next row (RS)** K18 (20: 22) and turn, leaving rem sts on a holder.

Work each side of neck separately.

Dec 1 st at neck edge of next 5 (6: 7) rows. 13 (14: 15) sts.

Work even until Front matches Back to shoulder bind-off, ending with RS facing for next row.

### SHAPE SHOULDER

Bind off.

With RS facing, slip center 16 (18: 20) sts onto a

holder, rejoin yarn to rem sts, K to end.

Complete to match first side, reversing shapings.

## Sleeves

### FIRST SECTION

Using size 6 (4mm) needles, cast on 18 (19: 20) sts.

Starting with a K row, work in st st for 12 rows, ending with RS facing for next row.**

Break off yarn and leave sts on a holder.

### SECOND SECTION

Work as given for First Section to **.

### JOIN SECTIONS

**Next row (RS)** K across 18 (19: 20) sts of Second Section, cast on 3 sts onto right needle, then with RS still facing K across 18 (19: 20) sts of First Section. 39 (41: 43) sts.

**Next row** Purl.

**Next row** K2, M1, K to last 2 sts, M1, K2.

Starting with a P row and working all increases as set by last row, work in st st, shaping sides by inc 1 st at each end of 4th row and every foll 4th row until there are 55 (57: 61) sts. Work even until Sleeve measures 6¼ (7½: 8¼)in/16 (19: 21)cm, ending with RS facing for next row.

### SHAPE TOP OF SLEEVE

Bind off 3 sts at beg of next 2 rows. 49 (51: 55) sts.

Working all decreases in same way as for armhole, dec 1 st at each end of next row and foll 3 alt rows.

Work 1 row, ending with RS facing for next row.

Bind off rem 41 (43: 47) sts.

## Finishing

Press lightly on WS following instructions on yarn label.

Sew both shoulder seams.

### NECK EDGING

With RS facing and using size 3 (3.25mm) circular needle, K across 13 (15: 17) sts on left back holder, pick up and knit 12 sts down left side of front neck, K across 16 (18: 20) sts on front holder, pick up and knit 12 sts up right side of front neck, then K across 13 (15: 17) sts on right back holder. 66 (72: 78) sts.

Work in garter st for 2 rows, ending with WS facing for next row.

Work picot bind-off as foll: bind off 3 sts (one st on right needle), *slip st on right needle back onto left needle, cast on 2 sts onto left needle, bind off 5 sts (one st on right needle), rep from * to end.

Sew sleeve seams.

### CUFF EDGINGS (both alike)

With RS facing and using size 3 (3.25mm) circular needle, starting and ending at cast-on sts where sections are joined, pick up and knit 10 sts along first row-end edge of cuff opening, 34 (36: 38) sts from original cast-on edge, then 10 sts along row-end edge of other side of opening. 54 (56: 58) sts.

**Row 1 (WS)** K10, M1, K34 (36: 38), M1, K10.

**Row 2** K11, M1, K34 (36: 38), M1, K11. 58 (60: 62) sts.

Work in garter st for 2 rows more, ending with WS facing for next row.

Work picot bind-off as foll: bind off 2 (3: 1) sts (one st on right needle), *slip st on right needle back onto left needle, cast on 2 sts onto left needle, bind off 5 sts (one st on right needle), rep from * to end, ending last rep by binding off 4 (5: 3) sts.

Sew row-end edges of Cuff Edgings to cast-on sts at top of sleeve opening.

### HEM EDGINGS (both alike)

With RS facing and using size 3 (3.25mm) needles, pick up and knit 76 (84: 92) sts along cast-on edge of Back (or Front).

Work picot bind-off as foll: bind off 3 (3: 4) sts (one st on right needle), *slip st on right needle back onto left needle, cast on 2 sts onto left needle, bind off 5 sts (one st on right needle), rep from * to end, ending last rep by binding off 6 (5: 6) sts.

## BOW STRIP

Using size 3 (3.25mm) needles, cast on 60 sts. Work picot bind-off as given for Neckband. Sew side seams, leaving Edgings free. Sew side seams of Edgings. Sew Sleeves into armholes. Make a button loop and attach button to ends of Neckband to fasten back neck opening. Tie Bow Strip into a bow and attach to center front neck as in photograph.

# girl's shoes

• • • • • • • • •

Anyone with a new baby on the way will be just thrilled to be given a little pair of baby shoes, and these are so pretty they are bound to earn you some brownie points. There are four variations on a theme here, so take your pick as to color and knit the basic shoes, then follow the instructions for the straps and/or edgings for the style you have chosen. Opt for the ballet slipper style to go with a party dress or a special robe, or for a more practical, but still really sweet, button-up design.

You can decorate the shoes if you choose with matching silk ribbons or rosettes, or a little bit of lace.

## To fit age, approximately

| 3–6 | 9–12 | 12–18 | months |
|---|---|---|---|

**Finished measurements**

LENGTH OF FOOT

| 4¼ | 5 | 6 | in |
|---|---|---|---|
| 11 | 13 | 15 | cm |

### Yarns

1 x 50g/1¾oz ball of Rowan *4 ply Cotton* in **MC** (white/
Bleached 113, gray/Ripple 121, pink/Orchid 120, or
beige/Opaque 112), and small amount for optional edging
in **CC** (Bleached 113 or Ripple 121)

### Needles

Pair of size 2 (3mm) knitting needles

### Extras

**White shoes:** 2 ribbon roses and 2 small pearl buttons
**Gray shoes:** Approximately 20 pearl beads and 2 heart-
shaped pearl buttons
**Pink shoes:** 2 ribbon rosebuds, 19½in/50cm of ⅛in/3mm
wide satin ribbon, and 63in/160cm of ⅜in/1cm wide
ribbon for ties
**Beige shoes:** Approximately 35–40 diamante stones

### Gauge

28 sts and 52 rows to 4in/10cm measured over seed st
using size 2 (3mm) needles *or size to obtain correct gauge.*

### Abbreviations

See page 117.

# basic shoes (make 2)

Using size 2 (3mm) needles and MC, cast on
21 (25: 29) sts.

**Row 1 (RS)** K1, *P1, K1, rep from * to end.

**Row 2** Inc in first st, P1, *K1, P1, rep from * to
last st, inc in last st. 23 (27: 31) sts.

These 2 rows form seed st and start shaping.

Work in seed st, inc 1 st at each end of 2nd row
and foll 3 (4: 5) alt rows. 31 (37: 43) sts.

Work 1 row, ending with WS facing for next row.

Dec 1 st at each end of next row and foll 4 (5: 6)
alt rows. 21 (25: 29) sts.

Work 1 row, ending with WS facing for next row.

**SHAPE HEEL**

Cast on 5 (6: 7) sts at beg of next row. 26 (31:
36) sts.

Inc 1 st at end of 2nd row and foll 4 (5: 6) alt
rows. 31 (37: 43) sts.

Work 1 row, ending with WS facing for next row.

Bind off 19 (21: 23) sts at beg and inc 1 st at end
of next row. 13 (17: 21) sts.

Work 10 (14: 18) rows, ending with RS facing for
next row.

Dec 1 st at beg of next row, then cast on 19 (21:
23) sts at beg of foll row. 31 (37: 43) sts.

Dec 1 st at beg of next row and foll 4 (5: 6) alt
rows. 26 (31: 36) sts.

Work 1 row, ending with RS facing for next row.

Bind off in seed st.

## Finishing

Do NOT press.

Sew together even row-end edges to form heel
seam. Sew upper to sole around shaped edges,
easing in fullness. Add straps and/or edgings.

## white shoes

**Straps** (make 2)

Using size 2 (3mm) needles and MC, cast on
15 (17: 19) sts.

Work in seed st as given for Basic Shoe for 1 row,
ending with WS facing for next row.

**Row 2 (WS)** Work 2 tog, yo (to make a buttonhole),
seed st to end.

Bind off in seed st.

Sew one end of Strap to foot opening edge
approximately ¾in/2cm back from row-end edge
of foot opening, and sew on button to outside of
foot to correspond with buttonhole in Strap.**

Sew ribbon rose to front of foot as in photograph.

## gray shoes

**Straps** (make 2)

Work as given for White Shoes to **, attaching
Straps approximately ⅜in/1cm back from row-end
edge of foot opening.

**Edgings (make 2)**

Using size 2 (3mm) needles and CC, cast on
4 sts.

**Row 1** K1, P3.

**Row 2** K1, M1, K1 tbl, M1, skp. 5 sts.

**Row 3** K1, P2, [K1, P1] twice into next st, P1. 8 sts.

**Row 4** Bind off 4 sts (one st on right needle), K1,
M1, skp. 4 sts.

These 4 rows form patt.

Work in patt for 16 (20: 24) rows more, ending with
RS facing for next row.

Bind off.

Using photograph as a guide, sew straight edge of

Edging to front of foot, starting and ending near edge of Strap. Sew on beads as in photograph.

## pink shoes

**Edgings** (make 2)
Using size 2 (3mm) needles and MC, cast on 4 sts.
***Work in patt as given for Edging of Gray Shoes until strip, unstretched, fits around entire foot opening edge of Shoe, ending after patt row 4. Bind off.
Join cast-on and bound-off ends of Edging, then sew straight row-end edge to foot opening edge of Shoe, matching edging seam to heel seam.***
Using photograph as a guide, thread narrower ribbon through edge of Edging, just inside scalloped edge, joining ends of ribbon at center back. Sew on ribbon rosebuds to front of foot. Cut wider ribbon into 4 equal lengths. Attach one end of each length to foot opening edge of Shoe approximately ¾in/2cm forward from heel seam, to form ankle tie.

## beige shoes

**Edgings** (make 2)
Using size 2 (3mm) needles and CC, cast on 4 sts.
Work as given for Edging of Pink Shoes from *** to ***.
Using photograph as a guide, sew diamante stones to Edging, positioning one stone on each scallop of Edging.

# baby holdall

• • • • • • • •

Made much like the wall hanging on page 94 and using motifs similar to those of the cushion and blanket on page 86, this simple fold-over baby holdall has lots of pockets for all those odds and ends you always need for diaper changes. Each little pocket on the three sections closes with its own button and flap.

The holdall is knitted in Rowan *Handknit Cotton* in a mixture of stockinette stitch and seed stitch, and it would make a really nice gift for a baby shower.

The version shown here has been designed in harmonizing blue and beige, but you could just as easily make a girly version in pink and pale gray.

## Size

The finished holdall is 30¼in/77cm wide and 13¾in/35cm tall when opened out.

## Yarns

2 x 50g/1¾oz balls of Rowan *Handknit Cotton* in each of **A** (Chime 204), **B** (Linen 205), and **D** (Ice Water 239), and 1 ball in each of **C** (Ecru 251) and **E** (Tope 253)

## Needles

Pair of size 6 (4mm) knitting needles
Size 6 (4mm) circular knitting needle

## Extras

4 buttons

## Gauge

20 sts and 28 rows to 4in/10cm measured over st st using size 6 (4mm) needles *or size to obtain correct gauge*.

## Abbreviations

See page 117.

## Heart pocket

### CENTER SECTION

Using size 6 (4mm) needles and B, cast on 33 sts.
Starting with a K row, work in st st for 14 rows, ending with RS facing for next row.
Twisting yarns together where they meet to avoid holes forming, join in D and place chart for heart as foll:
**Row 15 (RS)** Using B K4, work next 25 sts as row 1 of chart for heart motif, using B K4.
**Row 16** Using B P4, work next 25 sts as row 2 of chart for heart motif, using B P4.
These 2 rows set position of chart.
Work as set until all 40 rows of chart have been completed,

ending with RS facing for next row.
Break off D and cont using B only.
**Work in st st for 14 rows, ending with RS facing for next row.
Bind off.

### BORDER

With RS facing, using size 6 (4mm) circular needle and C, pick up and knit 33 sts evenly along cast-on edge, place marker on needle, 49 sts up first row-end edge, place 2nd marker on needle, 33 sts along bound-off edge, place 3rd marker on needle, then 49 sts along other row-end edge, place 4th marker on needle. 164 sts.
**Round 1 (RS)** *[K1, P1] to within 1 st of marker, K1, slip marker onto right needle, rep from * to end.
**Round 2** *Inc in next st, [P1, K1] to within 2 sts of marker, P1, inc in next st, slip marker onto right needle, rep from * to end. 172 sts.
Rep last 2 rounds twice more. 188 sts.
Bind off.

## Star pocket

Work as given for Heart Pocket, but working from chart for star in place of chart for heart.

## Moon pocket

### CENTER SECTION

Using size 6 (4mm) needles and A, cast on 33 sts.
Starting with a K row, work in st st for 14 rows, ending with RS facing for next row.
Twisting yarns together where they meet to avoid holes forming, join in B and place chart for moon as foll:
**Row 15 (RS)** Using A K4, work next 25 sts as row 1 of chart for moon motif, using A K4.
**Row 16** Using A P4, work next 25 sts as row 2 of chart for moon motif, using A P4.
These 2 rows set position of chart.

Work as set until all 40 rows of chart have been completed, ending with RS facing for next row.

Break off B and cont using A only.

Complete as given for Heart Pocket from **.

## Heart outer panel

### CENTER SECTION

Using size 6 (4mm) needles and A, cast on 41 sts.

Starting with a K row, work in st st for 20 rows, ending with RS facing for next row.

Twisting yarns together where they meet to avoid holes forming, join in B and place chart for heart as foll:

**Row 21 (RS)** Using A K8, work next 25 sts as row 1 of chart for heart motif, using A K8.

**Row 22** Using A P8, work next 25 sts as row 2 of chart for heart motif, using A P8.

These 2 rows set position of chart.

Work as set until all 40 rows of chart have been completed, ending with RS facing for next row.

Break off B and cont using A only.

***Work in st st for 20 rows, ending with RS facing for next row.

Bind off.

### BORDER

With RS facing, using size 6 (4mm) circular needle and D, pick up and knit 41 sts evenly along cast-on edge, place

**HEART MOTIF**

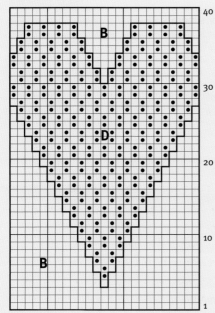

**MOON MOTIF**

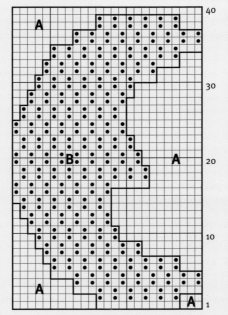

**STAR MOTIF**

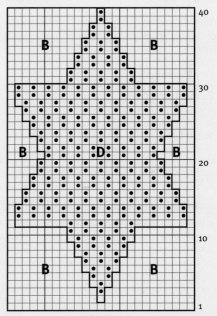

## KEY

☐ K on RS, P on WS

☑ P on RS, K on WS

marker on needle, 59 sts up first row-end edge, place 2nd marker on needle, 41 sts along bound-off edge, place 3rd marker on needle, then 59 sts along other row-end edge, place 4th marker on needle. 200 sts.

**Round 1 (RS)** *[K1, P1] to within 1 st of marker, K1, slip marker onto right needle, rep from * to end.

**Round 2** *Inc in next st, [P1, K1] to within 2 sts of marker, P1, inc in next st, slip marker onto right needle, rep from * to end. 208 sts.

Rep last 2 rounds 4 times more. 240 sts.

Bind off.

## Star outer panel

Work as given for Heart Outer Panel, but working from chart for star in place of chart for heart.

## Moon outer panel

### CENTER SECTION

Using size 6 (4mm) needles and B, cast on 41 sts.

Starting with a K row, work in st st for 20 rows, ending with RS facing for next row.

Twisting yarns together where they meet to avoid holes forming, join in D and place chart for moon as foll:

**Row 21 (RS)** Using B K8, work next 25 sts as row 1 of chart for moon motif, using B K8.

**Row 22** Using B P8, work next 25 sts as row 2 of chart for moon motif, using B P8.

These 2 rows set position of chart.

Work as set until all 40 rows of chart have been completed, ending with RS facing for next row.

Break off D and cont using B only.

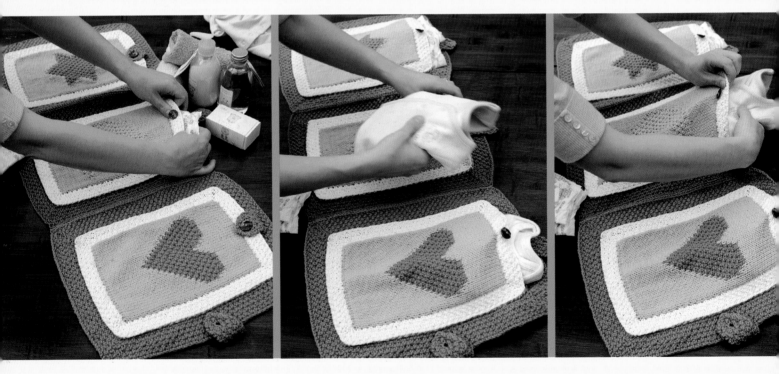

*gallery of projects*

Complete as given for Heart Outer Panel from ***, but using E in place of D.

## Buttonhole tabs (make 4)

Using size 6 (4mm) needles and D, cast on 9 sts.

**Row 1 (RS)** K1, [P1, K1] 4 times.

**Rows 2 and 3** P1, [K1, P1] 4 times.

**Row 4** As row 1.

These 4 rows form patt.

Work in patt for 9 rows more, ending with WS facing for next row.

**Row 14 (WS)** Patt 4 sts, yo, work 2 tog (to make a buttonhole), patt 3 sts.

Keeping patt correct, dec 1 st at each end of next 3 rows, ending with WS facing for next row. 3 sts.

**Next row (WS)** K3tog and fasten off.

## Finishing

Press lightly on WS following instructions on yarn label. Using photograph as a guide, sew Outer Panels together to form one long strip. Sew Pockets to WS of Outer Panels along lower and side edges. Sew on a button to top edge of each Pocket, then sew a Buttonhole Tab to each Outer Panel along border pick-up row to fasten pockets. Sew on rem Buttonhole Tab to one end of joined Outer Panels, fold holdall in three, then sew on 4th button to fasten with this Buttonhole Tab.

# sleeveless top

• • • • • • • • • •

This little retro-style top is just the thing for wearing with jeans and a shirt, and is usefully unisex. It is very simple to knit so even relative beginners can master this one easily. The little pocket feature on the front provides an eyecatching finishing touch.

If you want to try a variation, work the cast-on on the back and front and the bind-off on the neckband in a contrasting color.

Knitted in Rowan *Calmer*, which is a double-knitting-weight yarn, it is quick to work, too.

**To fit age, approximately**

| 3–6 | 6–9 | 9–12 | 12–18 | 18–24 | months |
|------|------|------|------|------|------|

**Finished measurements**

AROUND CHEST

| 19½ | 21¼ | 22¾ | 24¾ | 26¾ | in |
|------|------|------|------|------|------|
| 50 | 54 | 58 | 63 | 68 | cm |

Length from shoulder

| 8¾ | 9½ | 10¼ | 11¾ | 13½ | in |
|------|------|------|------|------|------|
| 22 | 24 | 26 | 30 | 34 | cm |

## Yarns

2 (2: 2: 3: 3) x 50g/1¾oz balls of Rowan *Calmer* in Khaki 474

## Needles

Pair of size 7 (4.5mm) knitting needles
Pair of size 8 (5mm) knitting needles

## Extras

6 (6: 6: 7: 7) buttons

## Gauge

21 sts and 30 rows to 4in/10cm measured over st st using
size 8 (5mm) needles *or size to obtain correct gauge.*

## Abbreviations

See page 117.

## Back

Using size 7 (4.5mm) needles, cast on 54 (58: 62: 66: 70) sts.
**Rib row 1 (RS)** K2, *P2, K2, rep from * to end.
**Rib row 2** P2, *K2, P2, rep from * to end.
These 2 rows form rib.
Work in rib for 4 (4: 4: 6: 6) rows more, ending with RS facing
for next row.
Change to size 8 (5mm) needles.
Starting with a K row, work in st st for 2 (4: 6: 8: 10) rows,
ending with RS facing for next row.**
**Next row (dec row) (RS)** K6, skp, K to last 4 sts, K2tog, K2.
***Work 7 (7: 7: 9: 9) rows.
Rep last 8 (8: 8: 10: 10) rows twice more, then first of these
rows (the dec row) again. 46 (50: 54: 58: 62) sts.
Work even until Back measures 4¾ (5: 5½: 6¾: 7¾)in/
12 (13: 14: 17: 20)cm, ending with RS facing for next row.

SHAPE ARMHOLES

Bind off 4 sts at beg of next row. 42 (46: 50: 54: 58) sts.
Work 1 row, placing marker at beg of row—this marker
denotes base of armhole.
**Next row (RS)** K2, skp, K to last 4 sts, K2tog, K2.
Working all armhole decreases as set by last row, dec 1 st
at each end of 4th row and 2 foll 4th rows. 34 (38: 42: 46:
50) sts.
Work even until armhole measures 3¼ (3½: 4: 4¼: 4¾)in/
8 (9: 10: 11: 12)cm, ending with RS facing for next row.

SHAPE BACK NECK

**Next row (RS)** K9 (10: 11: 12: 13) and turn, leaving rem sts
on a holder.
Work each side of neck separately.
Dec 1 st at neck edge of next 2 rows. 7 (8: 9: 10: 11) sts.
Work 1 row, ending with RS facing for next row.

SHAPE SHOULDER

Bind off.
With RS facing, slip center 16 (18: 20: 22: 24) sts onto a
holder, rejoin yarn to rem sts, K to end.
Complete to match first side, reversing shapings.

## Front

Work as given for Back to **.
**Next row (RS)** K2, skp, K to last 8 sts, K2tog, K6.
Now work as given for Back from *** to start of armhole
shaping.

SHAPE ARMHOLES

Work 1 row, placing marker at beg of row—this marker

denotes base of armhole.

Bind off 4 sts at beg of next row. 42 (46: 50: 54: 58) sts.

Working all armhole decreases as set by Back, dec 1 st at each end of next row and 3 foll 4th rows. 34 (38: 42: 46: 50) sts.

Work even until armhole measures 2¼ (2¾: 3¼: 3½: 4)in/6 (7: 8: 9: 10)cm, ending with RS facing for next row.

### SHAPE FRONT NECK

**Next row (RS)** K12 (13: 14: 15: 16) and turn, leaving rem sts on a holder.

Work each side of neck separately.

Dec 1 st at neck edge of next 5 rows. 7 (8: 9: 10: 11) sts.

Work 4 rows, ending with RS facing for next row.

### SHAPE SHOULDER

Bind off.

With RS facing, slip center 10 (12: 14: 16: 18) sts onto a holder, rejoin yarn to rem sts, K to end.

Complete to match first side, reversing shapings.

## Finishing

Press lightly on WS following instructions on yarn label.

### FRONT NECKBAND

With RS facing and using size 7 (4.5mm) needles, pick up and knit 10 (9: 10: 9: 10) sts down left side of neck, K across 10 (12: 14: 16: 18) sts on front holder, then pick up and knit 10 (9: 10: 9: 10) sts up right side of neck. 30 (30: 34: 34: 38) sts.

Starting with rib row 2, work in rib as given for Back for 3 rows, ending with RS facing for next row.

Bind off in rib.

### BACK NECKBAND

With RS facing and using size 7 (4.5mm) needles, pick up and knit 3 (4: 3: 4: 3) sts down right side of neck, K across 16 (18: 20: 22: 24) sts on back holder, then pick up and knit 3 (4: 3: 4: 3) sts up left side of neck. 22 (26: 26: 30: 30) sts.

Starting with rib row 2, work in rib as given for Back for 3 rows, ending with RS facing for next row.

Bind off in rib.

Sew right side seam.

### RIGHT ARMHOLE BORDER

Using size 7 (4.5mm) needles, cast on 7 sts.

**Rib row 1 (RS)** K2, *P1, K1, rep from * to last st, K1.

**Rib row 2** K1, *P1, K1, rep from * to end.

These 2 rows form rib.

Work in rib until Right Armhole Border, when slightly stretched, fits around entire right armhole edge, starting and ending at shoulder bind-off and ending with RS facing for next row.

Bind off in rib.

Slip stitch Border in place.

### LEFT FRONT ARMHOLE BORDER

Work as given for Right Armhole Border until this Border, when slightly stretched, fits along left front armhole edge, between marker at underarm and shoulder bind-off and ending with RS facing for next row.

Bind off in rib.

Slip stitch Border in place.

### LEFT BACK ARMHOLE BORDER

Work to match Left Front Armhole Border.

### LEFT BACK BUTTON BORDER

Using size 7 (4.5mm) needles, cast on 9 sts.

Work in rib as given for Right Armhole Border until this Border, when slightly stretched, fits up left back side seam edge, from cast-on edge to top of Left Back Armhole Border and ending with RS facing for next row.

Bind off in rib.

Slip stitch Border in place.

Mark positions for 4 (4: 4: 5: 5) buttons on this Border—first to come 1¹/₈in/3cm up from cast-on edge, last to come 1¹/₈in/3cm down from bound-off edge, and rem 2 (2: 2: 3: 3) buttons evenly spaced between.

### LEFT FRONT BUTTONHOLE BORDER

Work to match Left Back Button Border **and at the same time** work 4 (4: 4: 5: 5) buttonholes to correspond with positions marked for buttons as foll:

**Buttonhole row (RS)** Rib 3, work 2 tog, yo (to make a buttonhole), rib 4.

Slip stitch Border in place.

Lay Left Front Buttonhole Border over Left Back Button Border and sew on buttons to correspond with buttonholes.

### RIGHT SHOULDER BORDER

Using size 7 (4.5mm) needles, cast on 7 sts.

Work in rib as given for Right Armhole Border until this Border, when slightly stretched, fits across entire right shoulder edge, from bound-off edge of Neckbands to row-end edges of Armhole Border and ending with RS facing for next row.

Bind off in rib.

Slip stitch Border in place to back and front shoulder edges.

### LEFT BACK SHOULDER BORDER

Work to match Right Shoulder Border.

Slip stitch Border in place to back shoulder edge.

Mark positions for 2 buttons on this Border—first to come ¾in/2cm up from cast-on edge, and second to come ¾in/2cm down from bound-off edge.

### LEFT FRONT SHOULDER BORDER

Work to match Left Back Shoulder Border **and at the same time** work 2 buttonholes to correspond with positions marked for buttons as foll:

**Buttonhole row (RS)** Rib 2, work 2 tog, yo (to make a buttonhole), rib 3.

Slip stitch Border in place to front shoulder edge.

Lay Left Front Shoulder Border over Left Back Shoulder Border and sew on buttons to correspond with buttonholes.

### POCKET

Using size 8 (5mm) needles, cast on 10 sts.

Work in rib as given for Back, shaping sides by inc 1 st at each end of 3rd row and foll 4 alt rows, taking inc sts into rib. 20 sts.

Work 11 rows, ending with RS facing for next row.

Bind off in rib.

**POCKET BORDER**

Using size 7 (4.5mm) needles, cast on 7 sts.

Work in rib as given for Right Armhole Border until this Border, when slightly stretched, fits across bound-off edge of Pocket, ending with RS facing for next row.

Bind off in rib.

Slip stitch Border in place to bound-off edge of Pocket.

Using photograph as a guide, sew Pocket onto Front.

# cushion and blanket

• • • • • • • • •

This patchwork nursery cushion and matching blanket alternative will light up any baby's bedroom with their storytale imagery—the man in the moon, two stars, and a heart. Knitted in a mixture of stockinette, garter, and seed stitches, they make interesting projects to work.

The blanket is made in exactly the same design as the cushion but with more patches, and is edged, like the cushion, with a striped garter stitch border.

The duo are very cozy, indeed, as they are knitted in Rowan's *Cashsoft* yarn.

# blanket

## Size
The finished blanket measures 37½in/95cm square.

## Yarns
5 x 50g/1¾oz balls of Rowan *RYC Cashsoft Baby DK* in **A** (Snowman 800) and 3 balls in each of **B** (Chicory 804) and **C** (Cloud 805)
5 x 50g/1¾oz balls of Rowan *RYC Cashsoft DK* in **D** (Mirage 503)

## Needles
Pair of size 6 (4mm) knitting needles
Size 6 (4mm) circular knitting needle

## Gauge
22 sts and 30 rows to 4in/10cm measured over st st using size 6 (4mm) needles *or size to obtain correct gauge*.

## Abbreviations
See page 117.

## Shooting star patch (make 4)
### CENTER SECTION
Using size 6 (4mm) needles and A, cast on 35 sts.
Starting with a K row, work in st st for 4 rows, ending with RS facing for next row.
Twisting yarns together where they meet to avoid holes forming, join in B and place chart for shooting star as foll:
**Row 5 (RS)** Using A K9, work next 17 sts as row 1 of chart for shooting star motif, using A K9.
**Row 6** Using A P9, work next 17 sts as row 2 of chart for shooting star motif, using A P9.
These 2 rows set position of chart.
**Work as set until all 40 rows of chart have been

completed, ending with RS facing for next row.
Break off B and cont using A only.
Work in st st for 4 rows, ending with RS facing for next row.
Bind off.

### BORDER
With RS facing, using size 6 (4mm) circular needle and C, pick up and knit 33 sts evenly along each edge of Center Section. 132 sts.
**Round 1 (RS)** *[K1, P1] 16 times, K1, rep from * to end.
**Round 2** *Inc in next st, [P1, K1] 15 times, P1, inc in next st, rep from * to end. 140 sts.
**Round 3** *[K1, P1] 17 times, K1, rep from * to end.
**Round 4** *Inc in next st, [P1, K1] 16 times, P1, inc in next st, rep from * to end. 148 sts.
**Round 5** *[K1, P1] 18 times, K1, rep from * to end.
**Round 6** *Inc in next st, [P1, K1] 17 times, P1, inc in next st, rep from * to end. 156 sts.
Break off C and join in D.
***Round 7** Knit.
**Round 8** [K1, M1, K37, M1, K1] 4 times. 164 sts.
**Round 9** Knit.
**Round 10** [K1, M1, K39, M1, K1] 4 times. 172 sts.
**Round 11** Knit.
**Round 12** [K1, M1, K41, M1, K1] 4 times. 180 sts.
Bind off.

## Star patch (make 4)
### CENTER SECTION
Using size 6 (4mm) needles and A, cast on 35 sts.
Starting with a K row, work in st st for 4 rows, ending with RS facing for next row.
Twisting yarns together where they meet to avoid holes forming, join in B and place chart for star as foll:
**Row 5 (RS)** Using A K6, work next 23 sts as row 1 of chart for star motif, using A K6.
**Row 6** Using A P6, work next 23 sts as row 2 of chart for star

## SHOOTING STAR MOTIF

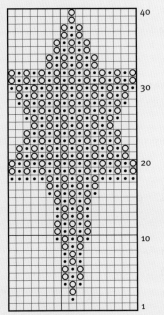

## STAR MOTIF

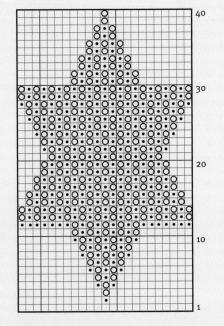

## MOON MOTIF

## HEART MOTIF

motif, using A P6.

These 2 rows set position of chart.
Complete as given for Shooting Star
Patch from **.

### Moon patch (make 4)

#### CENTER SECTION

Using size 6 (4mm) needles and A,
cast on 35 sts.

Starting with a K row, work in st st
for 4 rows, ending with RS facing for
next row.

Twisting yarns together where they
meet to avoid holes forming, join in C
and place chart for moon as foll:

**Row 5 (RS)** Using A K5, work next 25
sts as row 1 of chart for moon motif,
using A K5.

**Row 6** Using A P5, work next 25 sts as
row 2 of chart for moon motif, using
A P5.

These 2 rows set position of chart.
****Work as set until all 40 rows of
chart have been completed, ending
with RS facing for next row.

Break off C and cont using A only.

Work in st st for 4 rows, ending with
RS facing for next row.

Bind off.

#### BORDER

With RS facing, using size 6 (4mm)
circular needle and B, pick up and knit
33 sts evenly along each edge of
Center Section. 132 sts.

**Round 1 (RS)** *[K1, P1] 16 times, K1,
rep from * to end.

**Round 2** *Inc in next st, [P1, K1] 15 times, P1, inc in next st, rep from * to end. 140 sts.

**Round 3** *[K1, P1] 17 times, K1, rep from * to end.

**Round 4** *Inc in next st, [P1, K1] 16 times, P1, inc in next st, rep from * to end. 148 sts.

**Round 5** *[K1, P1] 18 times, K1, rep from * to end.

**Round 6** *Inc in next st, [P1, K1] 17 times, P1, inc in next st, rep from * to end. 156 sts.

Break off B and join in D.

Complete as given for Shooting Star Patch from ***.

**Heart patch** (make 4)

**CENTER SECTION**

Using size 6 (4mm) needles and A, cast on 35 sts.

Starting with a K row, work in st st for 4 rows, ending with RS facing for next row.

Twisting yarns together where they meet to avoid holes forming, join in C and place chart for heart as foll:

**Row 5 (RS)** Using A K5, work next 25 sts as row 1 of chart for heart motif, using A K5.

**Row 6** Using A P5, work next 25 sts as row 2 of chart for heart motif, using A P5.

These 2 rows set position of chart.

Complete as given for Moon Patch from ****.

## Finishing

Press patches lightly on WS following instructions on yarn label.

Arrange patches in four rows of four patches, from top to bottom and left to right as foll:

**1st row**—star, heart, star, heart.

**2nd row**—moon, shooting star, moon, shooting star.

**3rd and 4th rows**—as 1st and 2nd rows.

Sew patches together in rows as arranged, then sew rows together.

BORDERS (all 4 alike)

With RS facing, using size 6 (4mm) circular needle and A, pick up and knit 180 sts evenly along one edge of joined Patches.

**Row 1 (WS)** Knit.

**Rows 2 and 3** K1, M1, K to last st, M1, K1. 184 sts.
Break off A and join in C.

**Rows 4 to 7** K1, M1, K to last st, M1, K1. 192 sts.
Break off C and join in B.

**Rows 8 to 11** K1, M1, K to last st, M1, K1. 200 sts.
Break off B and join in D.

**Rows 12 to 15** K1, M1, K to last st, M1, K1. 208 sts.
Bind off.

Sew shaped row-end edges of Borders together at corners.


# cushion

## Size

The finished cover fits a 16in/40cm square pillow form.

## Yarns

2 x 50g/1¾oz balls of Rowan *RYC Cashsoft Baby DK* in each of **A** (Snowman 800), **B** (Chicory 804), and **C** (Cloud 805)
3 x 50g/1¾oz balls of Rowan *RYC Cashsoft DK* in **D** (Mirage 503)

## Needles

Pair of size 6 (4mm) knitting needles

## Extras

16in/40cm square pillow form

## Gauge

22 sts and 30 rows to 4in/10cm measured over st st using size 6 (4mm) needles *or size to obtain correct gauge.*

## Abbreviations

See page 117.

## Shooting star patch

Work as given for Shooting Star Patch of Blanket on page 88.

## Star patch

Work as given for Star Patch of Blanket on pages 88 and 90.

## Moon patch

Work as given for Moon Patch of Blanket on pages 90 and 91.

## Heart patch

Work as given for Heart Patch of Blanket on page 91.

## Back

Using size 6 (4mm) needles and D, cast on 90 sts.
Starting with a K row, work in st st for 16in/40cm, ending with RS facing for next row.
Bind off.

## Finishing

Press patches on WS lightly following instructions on yarn label.

Using photograph as a guide, sew Patches together to form

one large square two Patches wide
and two Patches long.

**BORDERS** (all 4 alike)
With RS facing, using size 6 (4mm)
needles and A, pick up and knit 90 sts
evenly along one edge of joined
Patches.
**Row 1 (WS)** Knit.
**Rows 2 and 3** K1, M1, K to last st, M1,
K1. 94 sts.
Break off A and join in C.
**Rows 4 to 7** K1, M1, K to last st, M1,
K1. 102 sts.
Break off C and join in B.
**Rows 8 to 11** K1, M1, K to last st, M1,
K1. 110 sts.
Break off B and join in D.
**Rows 12 to 15** K1, M1, K to last st,
M1, K1. 118 sts.
Bind off.
Sew shaped row-end edges of Borders
together at corners.
Sew Back to WS of joined Patches
level with Border pick-up row (so that
Border remains free), leaving one side
open. Insert pillow form and sew
fourth side closed.

# wall hanging

• • • • • • • • •

This is a great project to knit because you work the little pockets separately, which makes them easy to take with you on the bus or work on in a waiting room. Once all the pockets are complete, you knit the backing in three panels and stitch on the pockets.

If you want to work the hanging to go with the holdall on page 74 or the cushion and blanket on page 86 as a gift set, simply choose matching colors.

Becauce it is knitted in very simple stitches, even a relative beginner could master this design, and it makes a handy introduction to using knitting charts.

## Size

The finished wall hanging is 32½in/83cm wide and 39¾in/101cm tall.

## Yarns

5 x 50g/1¾oz balls of Rowan *Handknit Cotton* in **H** (Shell 310), 4 balls in **C** (Linen 205), 3 balls in each of **A** (Bermuda 324) and **D** (Bleached 263), 2 balls in each of **B** (Celery 309), **F** (Lupin 305), and **G** (Sugar 303), and 1 ball in **E** (Seafarer 318)

## Needles

Pair of size 6 (4mm) knitting needles
Size 6 (4mm) circular knitting needle

## Gauge

20 sts and 28 rows to 4in/10cm measured over st st using size 6 (4mm) needles *or size to obtain correct gauge.*

## Abbreviations

See page 117.

## Heart pockets (make 3)

### CENTER SECTION

Using size 6 (4mm) needles and D, cast on 33 sts.
Starting with a K row, work in st st for 10 rows, ending with RS facing for next row.
Twisting yarns together where they meet to avoid holes forming, join in B and place chart for heart as foll:
**Row 11 (RS)** Using D K4, work next 25 sts as row 1 of chart for heart motif, using D K4.
**Row 12** Using D P4, work next 25 sts as row 2 of chart for heart motif, using A P4.
These 2 rows set position of chart.
Work as set until all 40 rows of chart have been completed, ending with RS facing for next row.
Break off B and cont using D only.

**Work in st st for 10 rows, ending with RS facing for next row.
Bind off.

### BORDER

With RS facing, using size 6 (4mm) circular needle and G, pick up and knit 33 sts evenly along cast-on edge, place marker on needle, 43 sts up first row-end edge, place 2nd marker on needle, 33 sts along bound-off edge, place 3rd marker on needle, then 43 sts along other row-end edge, place 4th marker on needle. 152 sts.
**Round 1 (RS)** *[K1, P1] to within 1 st of marker, K1, slip marker onto right needle, rep from * to end.
**Round 2** *Inc in next st, [P1, K1] to within 2 sts of marker, P1, inc in next st, slip marker onto right needle, rep from * to end. 160 sts.
Rep last 2 rounds twice more. 176 sts.
Bind off.**
Make a 2nd Heart Pocket, but using E in place of B.
Make a 3rd Heart Pocket, but using B in place of D, E in place of B, and F in place of G.

## Four-petal flower pockets (make 2)

### CENTER SECTION

Using size 6 (4mm) needles and D, cast on 33 sts.
Starting with a K row, work in st st for 10 rows, ending with RS facing for next row.
Twisting yarns together where they meet to avoid holes forming, join in B and E as required and place chart for four-petal flower as foll:
**Row 11 (RS)** Using D K4, work next 25 sts as row 1 of chart for four-petal flower motif, using D K4.
**Row 12** Using D P4, work next 25 sts as row 2 of chart for four-petal flower motif, using D P4.
These 2 rows set position of chart.
Work as set until all 40 rows of chart have been completed, ending with RS facing for next row.
Break off B and E and cont using D only.

## HEART MOTIF

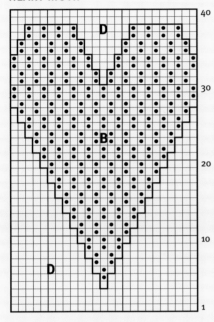

## FOUR-PETAL FLOWER MOTIF

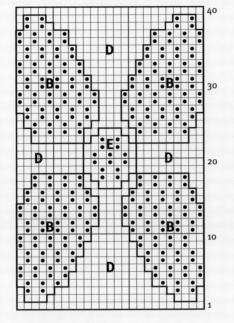

## STAR MOTIF

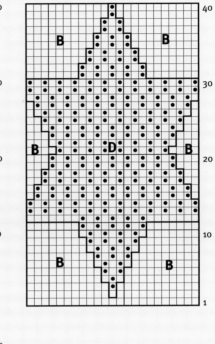

## SIX-PETAL FLOWER MOTIF

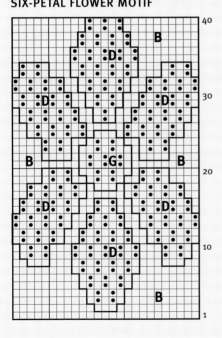

## BUTTERFLY MOTIF

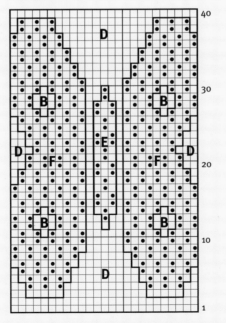

### KEY

☐ K on RS, P on WS

⊡ P on RS, K on WS

Complete as given for Heart Pockets from ** to **.
Make a 2nd Four-petal Flower Pocket, but using F in place of B, and B in place of E.

## Star pockets (make 2)
### CENTER SECTION
Using size 6 (4mm) needles and B, cast on 33 sts.
Starting with a K row, work in st st for 10 rows, ending with RS facing for next row.
Twisting yarns together where they meet to avoid holes forming, join in D and place chart for star as foll:

**Row 11 (RS)** Using B K5, work next 23 sts as row 1 of chart for star motif, using B K5.
**Row 12** Using B P5, work next 23 sts as row 2 of chart for star motif, using B P5.
These 2 rows set position of chart.
Work as set until all 40 rows of chart have been completed, ending with RS facing for next row.
Break off D and cont using B only.
Complete as given for Heart Pockets from ** to **, but using F in place of G.
Make a 2nd Star Pocket, but using E in place of D.

## Six-petal flower pocket
### CENTER SECTION
Using size 6 (4mm) needles and B, cast on 33 sts.
Starting with a K row, work in st st for 10 rows, ending with RS facing for next row.
Twisting yarns together where they meet to avoid holes forming, join in D and G as required and place chart for six-petal flower as foll:
**Row 11 (RS)** Using B K4, work next 25 sts as row 1 of chart for six-petal flower motif, using B K4.
**Row 12** Using B P4, work next 25 sts as row 2 of chart for six-petal flower motif, using B P4.
These 2 rows set position of chart.
Work as set until all 40 rows of chart have been completed, ending with RS facing for next row.
Break off D and G and cont using B only.
Complete as given for Heart Pockets from ** to **, but using F in place of G.

## Butterfly pocket
### CENTER SECTION
Using size 6 (4mm) needles and D, cast on 33 sts.
Starting with a K row, work in st st for 10 rows, ending with RS facing for next row.

Twisting yarns together where they meet to avoid holes forming, join in F, B, and E as required and place chart for butterfly as foll:

**Row 11 (RS)** Using D K4, work next 25 sts as row 1 of chart for butterfly motif, using D K4.

**Row 12** Using D P4, work next 25 sts as row 2 of chart for butterfly motif, using D P4.

These 2 rows set position of chart.

Work as set until all 40 rows of chart have been completed, ending with RS facing for next row.

Break off F, B, and E and cont using D only.

Complete as given for Heart Pockets from ** to **.

## Side panels (make 2)

Using size 6 (4mm) needles and H, cast on 53 sts.

Starting with a K row, work in st st for 84 rows, ending with RS facing for next row.

Break off H and join in C.

Work in st st for 84 rows more.

Break off C and join in H.

Work in st st for 84 rows more, ending with RS facing for next row.

Bind off.

## Center panel

Work as given for Side Panels, but using C in place of H, and H in place of C.

## Finishing

Press lightly on WS following instructions on yarn label.

Using photograph as a guide, sew Side Panels to either side of Center Panel.

### SIDE BORDERS (both alike)

With RS facing, using size 6 (4mm) circular needle and A, pick up and knit 189 sts evenly along one row-end edge of one Side Panel.

**Row 1 (WS)** K1, *P1, K1, rep from * to end.

**Row 2** Inc in first st, *K1, P1, rep from * to last 2 sts, K1, inc in last st. 191 sts.

Rep last 2 rows 5 times more. 201 sts.

Bind off.

### TOP AND BOTTOM BORDERS (both alike)

With RS facing, using size 6 (4mm) circular needle and A, pick up and knit 153 sts evenly along top (or bottom) edge of Panels.

**Row 1 (WS)** K1, *P1, K1, rep from * to end.

**Row 2** Inc in first st, *K1, P1, rep from * to last 2 sts, K1, inc in last st. 155 sts.

Rep last 2 rows 5 times more. 165 sts.

Bind off.

Sew shaped row-end edges of Borders together at corners.

Using photograph as a guide, sew Pockets onto Center and Side Panels, stitching along side and lower edges of each Pocket and leaving top edge open.

# rompers
# and hat

• • • • • • • • • •

This all-in-one suit can be knitted in two versions: a plain one in stockinette stitch and a textured one. The simple button-up style slips on very easily, and with its low V-neck front, it is ideal of wearing over a little undershirt. The yarn used is the cool and elastic Rowan *4 ply Cotton*, so it will feel comfortable next to the baby's skin and also offer plenty of stretch for ease of movement.

   Although the plain suit is shown in pink for a girl, and the textured version in blue for a boy, you can make your own choices on the colors. Knit the textured hat to accessorize either suit, working it with stripes on the fold-up brim as instructed or all in one color.

# rompers

## To fit age, approximately

| 0–3 | 3–6 | months |
|---|---|---|

## Finished measurements

### AROUND CHEST

| 20¾ | 22½ | in |
|---|---|---|
| 53 | 57 | cm |

### LENGTH FROM SHOULDER

| 17¼ | 18½ | in |
|---|---|---|
| 44 | 47 | cm |

### SLEEVE SEAM

| 1 | 1 | in |
|---|---|---|
| 3 | 3 | cm |

## Yarns

### PLAIN VERSION

3 x 50g/1¾oz balls of Rowan *4 ply Cotton* in Orchard 120

### TEXTURED VERSION

3 x 50g/1¾oz balls of Rowan *4 ply Cotton* in Bluebell 136

## Needles

Pair of size 2 (2.75mm) knitting needles
Pair of size 3 (3.25mm) knitting needles

## Extras

12 small buttons

## Gauge

28 sts and 38 rows to 4in/10cm measured over st st using size 3 (3.25mm) needles *or size to obtain correct gauge*.

## Abbreviations

See page 117.

## Body

### LEFT LEG

Using size 2 (2.75mm) needles, cast on 41 (45) sts.

**Rib row 1 (RS)** P1, *K1, P1, rep from * to end.

**Rib row 2** K1, *P1, K1, rep from * to end.

These 2 rows form rib.

Work in rib for 3 rows more, ending with WS facing for next row.

**Rib row 6 (WS)** Rib 2 (6), M1, *rib 4 (3), M1, rep from * to last 3 (6) sts, rib to end. 51 (57) sts.

Change to size 3 (3.25mm) needles.

### TEXTURED VERSION ONLY

Work in patt as foll:

**Row 1 (RS)** Knit.

**Row 2** Purl.

**Row 3** K1, [K1, yo, K1] all into next st, *sl 1, [K1, yo, K1] all into next st, rep from * to last st, K1.

**Row 4** K1, K3tog tbl, *sl 1, K3tog tbl, rep from * to last st, K1.

**Rows 5 and 6** As rows 1 and 2.

These 6 rows form patt.

Keeping patt correct throughout, work in patt, shaping leg by inc 1 st at each end of next row and every foll alt row until there are 83 (89) sts, taking inc sts into patt.

### PLAIN VERSION ONLY

Starting with a K row, work in st st, shaping leg by inc 1 st at each end of 7th row and every foll alt row until there are 83 (89) sts.

### BOTH VERSIONS

Work even until Leg measures 6 (6¼)in/15 (16)cm, ending with RS facing for next row.

### SHAPE CROTCH

Bind off 4 sts at beg of next 2 rows. 75 (81) sts.

Dec 1 st at each end of next row and foll 5 alt rows. 63 (69) sts.

Work 1 row, ending with RS facing for next row.**

Break off yarn and leave sts on a holder.

### RIGHT LEG

Work as given for Left Leg to **.

### JOIN LEGS

With RS facing, work across first
62 (68) sts of Right Leg, K tog last st
of Right Leg with first st of Left Leg,
then work across rem 62 (68) sts of
Left Leg. 125 (137) sts.
Work even until body measures
11 (11¾)in/28 (30)cm from cast-on
edge, ending with RS facing for
next row.

### SHAPE FOR FRONT OPENING

Bind off 3 sts at beg of next 2 rows.
119 (131) sts.
Work even until body measures
approximately 2¾in/7cm from
base of front opening, ending after
patt row 4 for textured version and
with RS facing for next row.

### DIVIDE FOR BACK AND FRONTS

**Next row (RS)** Patt 26 (29) sts and slip
these sts onto a holder for right front,
bind off 4 sts, patt until there are 59
(65) sts on right needle after bind-off
and slip these sts onto another holder
for back, bind off 4 sts, patt to end.
Work on this last set of 26 (29) sts
only for left front.

### SHAPE LEFT FRONT

Work 1 row, ending with RS facing for
next row.
**Next row (RS)** K2, skp, patt to end.
**Next row** Patt to last 3 sts, P3.
Rep last 2 rows 7 (8) times more. 18
(20) sts.

## SHAPE FRONT SLOPE

**Next row (RS)** K2, skp, patt to last 3 sts, K2tog, K1.

**Next row** P2, patt to last 3 sts, P3.

Rep last 2 rows 5 (6) times more. 6 sts.

**Next row (RS)** K2, sk2p, K1.

**Next row** P4.

**Next row** K1, sk2p.

**Next row** P2.

**Next row** K2tog and fasten off.

## SHAPE BACK

With WS facing, rejoin yarn to 59 (65) sts on back holder, patt to end.

**Next row (RS**) K2, skp, patt to last 4 sts, K2tog, K2.

**Next row** P3, patt to last 3 sts, P3.

Rep last 2 rows 14 (16) times more, and then first of these rows again, ending with WS facing for next row. 27 (29) sts.

Change to size 2 (2.75mm) needles.

Starting with rib row 2, work in rib as given for Left Leg for 5 rows (for back neckband), ending with RS facing for next row.

Bind off in rib.

## SHAPE RIGHT FRONT

With WS facing, rejoin yarn to 26 (29) sts on right front holder, patt to end.

**Next row (RS)** Patt to last 4 sts, K2tog, K2.

**Next row** P3, patt to end.

Rep last 2 rows 7 (8) times more. 18 (20) sts.

## SHAPE FRONT SLOPE

**Next row (RS)** K1, skp, patt to last 4 sts, K2tog, K2.

**Next row** P3, patt to last 2 sts, P2.

Rep last 2 rows 5 (6) times more. 6 sts.

**Next row (RS)** K1, K3tog, K2.

**Next row** P4.

**Next row** K3tog, K1.

**Next row** P2.

**Next row** K2tog and fasten off.

## Sleeves

Using size 2 (2.75mm) needles, cast on 55 (61) sts.

Work in rib as given for Left Leg for 6 rows, ending with RS facing for next row.

Change to size 3 (3.25mm) needles.

### TEXTURED VERSION ONLY

Starting with patt row 1 and keeping patt correct throughout, work in patt as given for Left Leg for 4 rows, ending with RS facing for next row.

### PLAIN VERSION ONLY

Starting with a K row, work in st st for 4 rows, ending with RS facing for next row.

### BOTH VERSIONS

### SHAPE RAGLAN

Bind off 3 sts at beg of next 2 rows. 49 (55) sts.

**Next row (RS)** K2, skp, patt to last 4 sts, K2tog, K2.

**Next row** P3, patt to last 3 sts, P3.

Rep last 2 rows 14 (16) times more, and then first of these rows again, ending with WS facing for next row. 17 (19) sts.

Change to size 2 (2.75mm) needles.

Starting with rib row 2, work in rib as given for Left Leg for 5 rows (for sleeve neckband), ending with RS facing for next row.

Bind off in rib.

## Finishing

Press lightly on WS following instructions on yarn label.

### BUTTON BORDER

With RS facing and using size 2 (2.75mm) needles, pick up and knit 43 (47) sts down left side of front neck, between fasten-off point and base of front opening.

Starting with rib row 2, work in rib as given for Left Leg for 5 rows, ending with RS facing for next row.

Bind off in rib.

### BUTTONHOLE BORDER

With RS facing and using size 2 (2.75mm) needles, pick up

and knit 43 (47) sts up right side of front neck, between base of front opening and fasten-off point.

Starting with rib row 2, work in rib as given for Left Leg for 2 rows, ending with WS facing for next row.

**Row 3 (WS)** Rib 14 (15), *work 2 tog, yo (to make a buttonhole), rib 5 (6), rep from * twice more, work 2 tog, yo (to make 4th buttonhole), rib 6.

Work in rib for 2 rows more, ending with RS facing for next row.

Bind off in rib.

Sew back crotch seam, from bound-off edge to where sections are joined. Sew front crotch seam, from bound-off edge to base of front opening. Lay Buttonhole Border over Button Border and sew together at base of opening. Sew sleeves seams. Sew Sleeves into armholes, matching top of sleeve seam to center of bound-off sts at underarm and bound-off edges at neck.

### BACK INSIDE LEG BUTTON BORDER

With RS facing and using size 2 (2.75mm) needles, starting and ending at cast-on edges, pick up and knit 42 (47) sts up first row-end edge to crotch seam, then 43 (48) sts down other row-end edge. 85 (95) sts.

Starting with rib row 1, work in rib as given for Left Leg for 3 rows, ending with RS facing for next row.

Bind off in rib.

### FRONT INSIDE LEG BUTTONHOLE BORDER

Work as given for Back Inside Leg Button Border, making buttonholes in row 2 as foll:

**Row 2 (RS)** Rib 4 (5), [work 2 tog, yo, rib 9 (10)] 3 times, work 2 tog, yo, rib 7 (9), yo, work 2 tog, [rib 9 (10), yo, work 2 tog] 3 times, rib 4 (5).

Sew on buttons to correspond with buttonholes.

## hat

### To fit age, approximately

| 0–3 | 3–6 | months |
|-----|-----|--------|

**Finished measurements**

**CIRCUMFERENCE AROUND HEAD**

| 13 | 14 | in |
|----|----|----|
| 33 | 36 | cm |

### Yarns

1 x 50g/1¾oz ball of Rowan 4 *ply Cotton* in each of **MC** (Bluebell 136 or Orchid 120) and **CC** (Bleached 113)

**Note:** For an alternative one-color hat, follow the instructions below, but use the same color yarn throughout.

### Needles

Pair of size 2 (2.75mm) knitting needles
Pair of size 3 (3.25mm) knitting needles

### Gauge

28 sts and 38 rows to 4in/10cm measured over st st using size 3 (3.25mm) needles *or size to obtain correct gauge.*

### Abbreviations

See page 117.

### Hat

Using size 2 (2.75mm) needles and MC, cast on 91 (101) sts.

**Rib row 1 (RS)** K1, *P1, K1, rep from * to end.

**Rib row 2** P1, *K1, P1, rep from * to end.

**Rib rows 3 to 6** As rows 1 and 2, twice.

Change to size 3 (3.25mm) needles.

Join in CC and work in patt as foll:

**Row 1 (RS)** Using CC, knit.

**Row 2** Using CC, purl.

**Rows 3 and 4** As rows 1 and 2.

**Row 5** Using MC, K1, [K1, yo, K1] all into next st, *sl 1, [K1, yo, K1] all into next st, rep from * to last st, K1.

**Row 6** Using MC, K1, K3tog tbl, *sl 1, K3tog tbl, rep from * to last st, K1.

These 6 rows form patt.

Work in patt for 16 rows more, ending after patt row 4 and with RS facing for next row.

Break off CC and cont using MC only.

Change to size 2 (2.75mm) needles.

**Next row (RS)** Knit (to form fold line).

Starting with a **K** row (to reverse RS of work), work in st st for 22 rows, ending with RS facing for next row.

Change to size 3 (3.25mm) needles.

Work 12 (16) rows more, ending with RS facing for next row.

**SHAPE CROWN**

**Row 1 (RS)** [K8, K2tog] 9 (10) times, K1. 82 (91) sts.

Work 1 row.

**Row 3** [K7, K2tog] 9 (10) times, K1. 73 (81) sts.

Work 1 row.

**Row 5** [K6, K2tog] 9 (10) times, K1. 64 (71) sts.

Work 1 row.

**Row 7** [K5, K2tog] 9 (10) times, K1. 55 (61) sts.

Work 1 row.

**Row 9** [K4, K2tog] 9 (10) times, K1. 46 (51) sts.

Work 1 row.

**Row 11** [K3, K2tog] 9 (10) times, K1. 37 (41) sts.

Work 1 row.

**Row 13** [K2, K2tog] 9 (10) times, K1. 28 (31) sts.

Work 1 row.

**Row 15** [K1, K2tog] 9 (10) times, K1. 19 (21) sts.

Work 1 row.

**Row 17** [K2tog] 9 (10) times, K1. 10 (11) sts.

Work 1 row.

Break off yarn and thread through rem 10 (11) sts. Pull up tight and fasten off securely.

**Finishing**

Press lightly on WS following instructions on yarn label.

Sew row-end edges together to form back seam, reversing seam below fold line row for turn-back. Fold turn-back to RS.

# heart card

• • • • • • • • • •

If you are planning a knitted gift for a newborn baby, then why not make a knitted motif card to go with it or perhaps add the same motif to the bag or box in which you present it? Don't forget to wrap your knitted gift in matching tissue paper, too.

It is really well worth taking a little extra time and trouble to show you care. And these small motifs will only take moments to make.

If you want to follow tradition, make a pink one for a girl or a blue one for a boy. Once you have knitted the motif, you just need to press it carefully and glue it to the chosen card, bag, or box.

## Size

The finished motif is 2in/5cm wide and 2¼in/6cm tall.

## Yarns

Small amount of Rowan *RYC Cashcotton 4 ply* in either Sugar 901 or Pretty 902

## Needles

Pair of size 3 (3.25mm) knitting needles

## Extras

Greeting card or gift bag
Approximately 30 small glass beads (optional)

## Gauge

28 sts and 36 rows to 4in/10cm measured over st st using size 3 (3.25mm) needles *or size to obtain correct gauge.*

## Abbreviations

See page 117.

## Motif

Using size 6 (4mm) needles, cast on 3 sts.
**Row 1 (WS)** K3.
**Row 2** K1, [M1, K1] twice. 5 sts.
**Row 3** K1, P to last st, K1.
**Row 4** K2, yo, skp, K1.
**Row 5** K1, P to last st, K1.
**Row 6** K2, yo, K to last 2 sts, yo, K2. 7 sts.
**Row 7** K1, P to last st, K1.
**Rows 8 to 13** As rows 6 and 7, 3 times. 13 sts.
**Row 14** K2, yo, K4, yo, skp, K3, yo, K2. 15 sts.
**Row 15** K1, P to last st, K1.
**Row 16** K1, skp, yo, K2, K2tog, yo, K1, yo, skp, K2, yo, K2tog, K1.
**Row 17** K1, P to last st, K1.
**Row 18** K1, skp, yo, sk2p, yo, K3, yo, K3tog, yo, K2tog, K1. 13 sts.
**Row 19** K1, P4, K3, P4, K1.
**Row 20** K1, skp, yo, skp, K1, [K2tog] twice, yo, K2tog, K1. 10 sts.

### DIVIDE FOR TOP

**Row 21 (WS)** K1, P2tog, P1, K1 and turn.
Work on these 4 sts only for first side of top.
**Row 22** K1, K2tog, lift first st on right needle over 2nd st, bind off rem st.
With WS facing, rejoin yarn to rem 5 sts and work as foll:
**Row 21 (WS)** K1, P1, P2tog tbl, K1. 4 sts.
**Row 22** K1, skp, lift first st on right needle over 2nd st, bind off rem st.

## Finishing

Press lightly on WS following instructions on yarn label.
If desired, sew on beads around outer edge of Motif.
Using photograph as a guide, attach Motif to greeting card or gift bag.

# practical
# information

• • • • • • • • • •

Most of the patterns in this book use only relatively simple knitting techniques and are suitable for beginners. A few designs provide a bit more of a challenge, to tempt intermediate and experienced knitters to show off their skills and to give beginners something to aim for.

The following knitting tips are reminders for knitters of all skill levels. If you take a little time to review them, you might find just the tip you need to give your knits the perfect professional-looking finish!

## gauge

To make a successful handknitted garment to the chosen size, it is essential that you work to the stated gauge—the correct number of stitches and rows over a 4in (10cm) square. To check that your own gauge is the same as that of the pattern, you need to make a small sample square approximately 5in (13cm) in size BEFORE you start to knit a pattern. You then smooth out the sample square, taking care not to stretch the fabric, and count the stitches and rows to 4in (10cm).

If there are fewer rows and stitches to 4in (10cm) than those specified in your pattern, you will need to use a size smaller needle to obtain the correct gauge. If there are too many stitches and rows on your sample, you will need to use a larger needle to obtain the correct gauge.

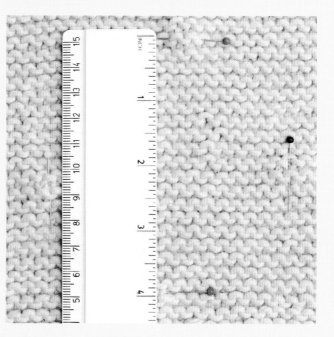

# finishing touches

There are a number of useful tips and techniques that will help ensure a professional finish on your garment.

## Blocking

When you have finished the various knitted pieces, they should usually be pressed. The knitting pattern explains whether to press and when to press. Check the yarn label as well for any pressing instructions.

Before pressing, pin out each piece (wrong side up) to the correct measurements—this is called "blocking." Place a clean, damp cloth on the knitting and press lightly, avoiding the ribbing or other raised textures such as cables.

## Seams

Most garment seams are worked in backstitch, which gives a tailored finish. For baby garments and delicate fabrics, you can also use a flat seam. For ribbing, use an invisible seam.

### BACKSTITCH SEAM

Place the two pieces of knitting right sides together, and pin in position. Sew together with a row of backstitches, worked one stitch in from the edge, as shown.

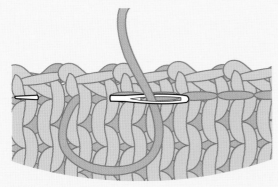

**Backstitch seam**

### FLAT SEAM

Place the two pieces of knitting right sides together, and pin in position. Sew together with overcasting stitches, matching ridge to ridge as shown.

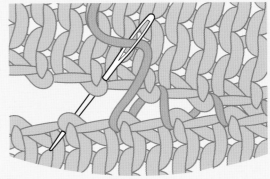

**Flat seam**

### INVISIBLE SEAM

This seam can be worked along row-ends if there is a knit stitch at each edge. With the right sides of the knitting facing you, place the two pieces of fabric side by side. Stitch together as shown, working along the center of a knit stitch on each edge.

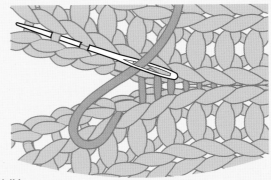

**Invisible seam**

## Button bands and buttonholes

If your garment has a separately worked buttonhole and button bands, first pin the fronts to the back at shoulders and sew the seams. Then pin the bands to the front, taking care to ensure that the lower edge of the garment forms a straight edge. Sew the bands in place, working one stitch in the band and one in the cardigan alternately.

### REINFORCED CARDIGAN BANDS

You can create a really professional finish on a cardigan by reinforcing the front bands with grosgrain-ribbon facings. First, pin a facing in place on the wrong side of each band, taking care not to stretch the knitting. Slip stitch the facings in place, as shown.

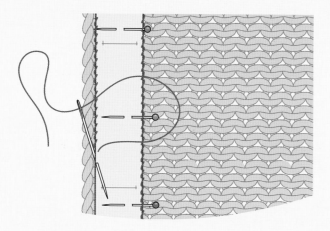

**Sewing on button band facing**

On the buttonhole band, cut the buttonholes in the facing to match the buttonholes on the knitting and work buttonhole stitch carefully around each one using a matching sewing thread.

Sew the buttons to the button band in corresponding positions, stitching through the knitting and the grosgrain ribbon facing.

### BUTTONHOLES

For very small buttonholes, a simple yarn-over eyelet is used. For larger buttonholes, you can make horizontal or vertical buttonholes. To knit a horizontal buttonhole, bind off one, two, or three stitches at the buttonhole position. On the next row, cast on the same number of stitches over those bound-off.

To make a vertical buttonhole, divide the stitches at the buttonhole position and work an equal number of rows on each set of stitches, then join up with a row of stitches worked right across both sections.

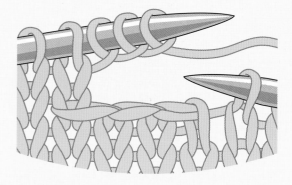

**Horizontal buttonhole**

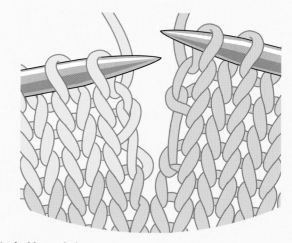

**Vertical buttonhole**

## Picking up and knitting stitches

When you work the neck trimming on a garment or borders on accessories, you will usually have to pick up and knit stitches along the edge of the knitting. The following tips help to create a tidy edging.

Stitches will have to be picked up along side edges of the knitting into the row-ends, or along cast-on or bound-off edges at the top and bottom of the knitting. Your pattern will tell you how many stitches to pick up and they should be picked up evenly along the edge for a smooth edging.

It is easiest to pick up stitches evenly if you divide the edge with pins. If you have 60 stitches to pick up, for example, along the front opening off a cardigan (along row-ends), you can divide this into 10 equal sections with pins and pick up six stitches in each section.

number of stitches in each section. Be sure to insert the knitting needle under both loops of each bound-off stitch, as shown, when picking up and knitting stitches along a bound-off edge—this will avoid loose stitches and holes.

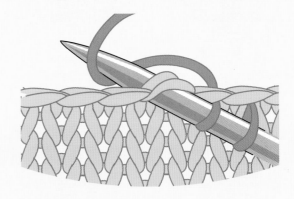

**Picking up stitches along bound-off edge**

## Picking up dropped stitches

If a stitch is accidentally dropped, it is easiest to use a crochet hook to pick it up, even if it has unraveled a few rows down.

To pick up knit stitches, insert the hook into the dropped stitch, catch the bar lying above the dropped stitch and pull it through. To pick up purl stitches, simply turn the work over and use the same method as for knit stitches.

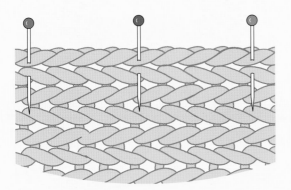

**Picking up stitches along row-ends**

To pick up and knit stitches, insert the right knitting needle through the edge of the knitting from the right side to the wrong side, wrap the yarn around the tip of the needle, and draw a loop through. Continue in this way all along the edge. The first row after the pick-up will be a wrong side row.

When picking up and knitting stitches along a bound-off or cast-on edge, first divide the edge into equal sections as shown above along a row-end edge. Then pick up an equal

## Joining in new yarn

Whenever possible, join a new ball of yarn at the beginning of a row. Where a new ball of yarn has to be joined in the middle of a row, you can make a neat join by splicing the yarn. Unravel a short length of the yarn from the old ball and the new one, and cut away a strand or two from each. Twist the remaining strands together to make one thickness of yarn. Knit carefully through this join, trimming off any stray ends.

# in the round

**Knitting on four needles**

If you prefer, you can knit baby hats or baby garments up to the armholes in a tube to eliminate the need for seams. To do this, you use four needles rather than two, spreading the knitting around three needles and using the fourth to knit with. Here are useful tips for casting-on onto three needles.

**1** Cast on the stitches onto one needle, then divide them evenly between the three needles.

**2** To start to knit, arrange the three needles in a triangle. The working yarn will be at the end of the third needle.

**3** Loosely knot a colored thread around the needle next to the working yarn to mark the start of the rounds. Then start to knit with the fourth needle, closing the cast-on triangle when knitting through the first stitch on the first needle.

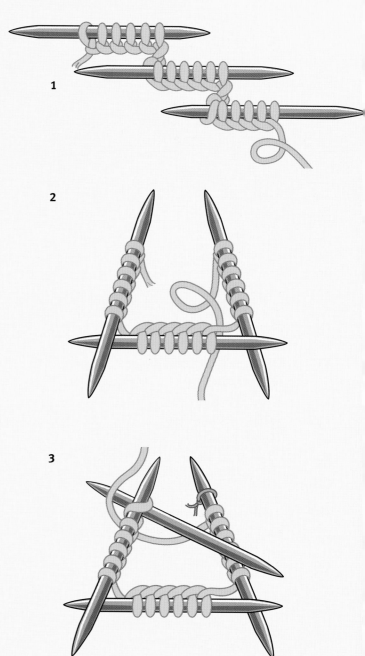

# working from patterns

## Knitting abbreviations

The abbreviations used in the patterns in this book are listed here. Any special abbreviations (such as those for cables) are given with individual patterns.

| | |
|---|---|
| **alt** | alternate |
| **beg** | begin(ning) |
| **CC** | contrasting color |
| **cm** | centimeter(s) |
| **cont** | continu(e)(ing) |
| **dec** | decreas(e)(ing) |
| **DK** | double knitting (a medium-weight yarn) |
| **foll** | follow(s)(ing) |
| **g** | gram(s) |
| **in** | inch(es) |
| **inc** | increas(e)(ing); increase one st by working into front and back of st |
| **K** | knit |
| **K2tog** | knit next 2 sts together |
| **m** | meter(s) |
| **M1** | make one st; pick up strand between st just knit and next st with tip of left needle and knit (or purl) into back of it |
| **M1P** | make one st; pick up strand between st just knit and next st with tip of left needle and purl into back of it |
| **MC** | main color |
| **mm** | millimeter(s) |
| **oz** | ounce(s) |
| **P** | purl |
| **P2tog** | purl next 2 sts together |
| **patt** | pattern; *or* work in pattern |
| **psso** | pass slipped stitch over |
| **rem** | remain(s)(ing) |
| **rep** | repeat(s)(ing) |
| **rev st st** | reverse stockinette stitch; purl sts on RS rows and knit sts on WS rows |
| **RS** | right side |
| **skp** | slip 1, knit 1, pass slipped st over st just knit (one st decreased) |
| **sk2p** | slip 1, knit 2 together, pass slipped st over st just knit together (2 sts decreased) |
| **sl** | slip |
| **st(s)** | stitch(es) |
| **st st** | stockinette stitch; knit sts on RS rows and purl sts on WS rows |
| **tbl** | through back of loop(s) |
| **tog** | together |
| **WS** | wrong side |
| **yd** | yard(s) |
| **yo** | yarn over needle (to make a new st on right needle) |

**\*** Repeat instructions after asterisk/s or between asterisk/s as many times as instructed.

**[ ]** Repeat instructions inside brackets as many times as instructed.

## Sizes in patterns

In patterns that have a choice of sizes, the smallest size comes first and the remaining sizes follow inside parentheses ( ). Where there is only one set of figures, it applies to all sizes. Be sure to follow the same size throughout the pattern.

# yarns

The following list covers the yarns used in this book. All the information was correct at the time of publication, but yarn companies change their products frequently and cannot absolutely guarantee that the yarn types or shades used will be available when you come to use these patterns.

For the best results, always use the yarn specified in your knitting pattern. Contact the distributors on page 120 to find a supplier of Rowan yarns near you. For countries not listed, contact the main office in the UK.

The yarn descriptions here will help you find an equivalent substitute if necessary. When assessing quantities of substitute yarns, always make sure you decide on the number of balls you need by ball length (yardage) rather than by ball weight.

Always check the yarn label for care instructions.

### ROWAN CALMER

A medium-weight cotton-mix yarn; 75 percent cotton, 25 percent acrylic/microfiber; approximately 175yd/160m per 50g/1¾oz ball; recommended gauge—21 sts and 30 rows to 4in/10cm measured over stockinette stitch using size 8 (5mm) knitting needles.

### ROWAN 4 PLY COTTON

A lightweight cotton yarn; 100 percent cotton; approximately 186yd/170m per 50g/1¾oz ball; recommended gauge—27–29 sts and 37–39 rows to 4in/10cm measured over stockinette stitch using size 2–3 (3–3.25mm) knitting needles.

### ROWAN 4 PLY SOFT

A lightweight wool yarn; 100 percent merino wool; approximately 191yd/175m per 50g/1¾oz ball; recommended gauge—28 sts and 36 rows to 4in/10cm measured over stockinette stitch using size 3 (3.25mm) knitting needles.

### ROWAN HANDKNIT COTTON

A medium-weight 100 percent cotton yarn; approximately 93yd/85m per 50g/1¾oz ball; recommended gauge—19–20 sts and 28 rows to 4in/10cm measured over stockinette stitch using size 6–7 (4–4.5mm) knitting needles.

### ROWAN RYC CASHCOTTON 4 PLY

A lightweight cotton-mix yarn; 35 percent cotton, 25 percent polyamide, 18 percent angora, 13 percent viscose, 9 percent cashmere; approximately 197yd/180m per 50g/1¾oz ball; recommended gauge—28 sts and 36 rows to 4in/10cm measured over stockinette stitch using size 3 (3.25mm) knitting needles.

### ROWAN RYC CASHSOFT BABY DK

A medium-weight wool-and-cashmere-mix yarn; 57 percent extra fine merino wool, 33 percent microfiber, 10 percent cashmere; approximately 142yd/130m per 50g/1¾oz ball; recommended gauge—22 sts and 30 rows to 4in/10cm measured over stockinette stitch using size 6 (4mm) knitting needles.

### ROWAN RYC CASHSOFT BABY 4 PLY

A lightweight wool-and-cashmere-mix yarn; 57 percent extra fine merino wool, 33 percent microfiber, 10 percent cashmere; approximately 197yd/180m per 50g/1¾oz ball; recommended gauge—28 sts and 36 rows to 4in/10cm measured over stockinette stitch using size 3 (3.25mm) knitting needles.

**ROWAN RYC CASHSOFT DK**

A medium-weight wool-and-cashmere-mix yarn; 57 percent extra fine merino wool, 33 percent microfiber, 10 percent cashmere; approximately 142yd/130m per 50g/1¾oz ball; recommended gauge—22 sts and 30 rows to 4in/10cm measured over stockinette stitch using size 6 (4mm) knitting needles.

**ROWAN RYC CASHSOFT 4 PLY**

A lightweight wool-and-cashmere-mix yarn; 57 percent extra fine merino wool, 33 percent microfiber, 10 percent cashmere; approximately 197yd/180m per 50g/1¾oz ball; recommended gauge—28 sts and 36 rows to 4in/10cm measured over stockinette stitch using size 3 (3.25mm) knitting needles.

**ROWAN WOOL COTTON**

A medium-weight wool-cotton-mix yarn; 50 percent merino wool and 50 percent cotton; approximately 123yd/113m per 50g/1¾oz ball; recommended gauge— 22–24 sts and 30–32 rows to 4in/10cm measured over stockinette stitch using size 5–6 (3.75–4mm) knitting needles.

## author's acknowledgments

I would like to thank the little children who modeled for this book, Amelia, Mia, and Ellie, their mums, and also my own daughter, Maddie. They were all stars! I would also like to thank Susan, John, and Anne for getting it together on the page, Penny and Sue for their knitting and pattern writing, Sally for her editing, and the team at Rowan for their support. I would also like to thank Julian and our children for their patience while we invaded the house with children and projects!

# yarn suppliers

Below is the list of overseas distributors for Rowan handknitting yarns; contact them for suppliers near you/in your country or contact the main office in the UK or the Rowan website for any others.

See pages 118 and 119 for yarn information.

**USA**
Westminster Fibers Inc.,
4 Townsend West, Suite 8, Nashua, NH 03063.
Tel: +1 (603) 886-5041/5043.
E-mail: rowan@westminsterfibers.com

**AUSTRALIA**
Australian Country Spinners, 314 Albert Street,
Brunswick, Victoria 3056.
Tel: (03) 9380 3888.
E-mail: sales@auspinners.com.au

**BELGIUM**
Pavan, Meerlaanstraat 73, B9860 Balegem
(Oosterzele).
Tel: (32) 9 221 8594.
E-mail: pavan@pandora.be

**CANADA**
Diamond Yarn, 9697 St Laurent, Montreal,
Quebec H3L 2N1.
Tel: (514) 388 6188.
Diamond Yarn (Toronto), 155 Martin Ross, Unit 3,
Toronto, Ontario M3J 2L9.
Tel: (416) 736-6111.
E-mail: diamond@diamondyarn.com

**FINLAND**
Coats Opti Oy, Ketjutie 3, 04220 Kerava.
Tel: (358) 9 274 871.
Fax: (358) 9 2748 7330.
E-mail: coatsopti.sales@coats.com

**FRANCE**
Elle Tricot, 8 Rue du Coq, 67000 Strasbourg.
Tel: (33) 3 88 23 03 13.
E-mail: elletricot@agat.net
www.elletricote.com

**GERMANY**
Wolle & Design, Wolfshovener Strasse 76,
52428 Julich-Stetternich.
Tel: (49) 2461 54735.
E-mail: Info@wolleunddesign.de
www.wolleunddesign.de
Coats GMbH, Eduardstrasse 44, D-73084 Salach.
Tel: (49) 7162/14-346. www.coatsgmbh.de

**HOLLAND**
de Afstap, Oude Leliestraat 12, 1015 AW
Amsterdam.
Tel: (31) 20 6231445.

**HONG KONG**
East Unity Co. Ltd., Unit B2,
7/F Block B, Kailey Industrial Centre,
12 Fung Yip Street, Chai Wan.
Tel: (852) 2869 7110.

**ICELAND**
Storkurinn, Laugavegi 59, 101 Reykjavik.
Tel: (354) 551 8258.
E-mail: malin@mmedia.is

**ITALY**
D.L. srl, Via Piave 24–26, 20016 Pero, Milan.
Tel: (39) 02 339 10 180.

**JAPAN**
Puppy Co. Ltd., T151-0051, 3-16-5 Sendagaya,
Shibuyaku, Tokyo.
Tel: (81) 3 3490 2827.
E-mail: info@rowan-jaeger.com

**KOREA**
Coats Korea Co. Ltd., 5F Kuckdong B/D, 935-40
Bangbae-Dong, Seocho-Gu, Seoul.
Tel: (82) 2 521 6262.
Fax: (82) 2 521 5181.

**NORWAY**
Coats Knappehuset A/S, Postboks 63, 2801
Gjovik.
Tel: (47) 61 18 34 00.

**SINGAPORE**
Golden Dragon Store, 101 Upper Cross Street
#02-51, People's Park Centre, Singapore.
Tel: (65) 6 5358454.

**SOUTH AFRICA**
Arthur Bales PTY, P.O. Box 44644, Linden 2104.
Tel: (27) 11 888 2401.

**SPAIN**
Oyambre, Pau Claris 145, 80009 Barcelona.
Tel: (34) 670 011957.
E-mail: comercial@oyambreonline.com

**SWEDEN**
Wincent, Norrtullsgatan 65, 113 45 Stockholm.
Tel: (46) 8 33 70 60.
E-mail: wincent@chello.se

**TAIWAN**
Laiter Wool Knitting Co. Ltd., 10-1 313 Lane, Sec
3, Chung Ching North Road, Taipei.
Tel: (886) 2 2596 0269.
Mon Cher Corporation, 9F No 117 Chung Sun First
Road, Kaoshiung. Tel: (886) 7 9711988.

**UK**
Rowan Yarns, Green Lane Mill,
Holmfirth, West Yorkshire HD9 2DX.
Tel: 01484 681881.
E-mail: mail@knitrowan.com
www.knitrowan.com